THE COMING RUSSIAN INVASION OF ISRAEL

UPDATED

THE COMING RUSSIAN INVASION OF ISRAEL
UPDATED

by

Thomas S. McCall & Zola Levitt

MOODY PRESS
CHICAGO

To
our beloved wives,
Carolyn McCall
and
Yvonne Levitt

© 1974, 1987 by
THE MOODY BIBLE INSTITUTE
OF CHICAGO

Library of Congress Cataloging in Publication Data

Levitt, Zola.
 The coming Russian invasion of Israel.

 McCall's name appears first on the earlier edition.
 1. Bible—Prophecies—Soviet Union. 2. Bible—Prophecies—Israel. I. McCall, Thomas S. II. Title.
BS649.R9L45 1987 224′.4015 87-1556
ISBN 0-8024-1624-1

4 5 6 7 8 Printing/LC/Year 93 92 91 90 89

Printed in the United States of America

Contents

Foreword to the 1987 Edition

No generation since the early years of the Christian church has had more reason to turn to the prophetic Word than those living in the twentieth century. In keeping with prophecy, Israel has moved back to her ancient land. Initial steps toward a world church and a world religion have already been taken. Many observers of the political scene believe that, in order to avoid nuclear suicide, all nations must unite into one world government.

With Israel back in her land and Russia boasting about having the greatest army in the world, Ezekiel 38 and 39 become extremely relevant. Those two chapters predict an invasion of Israel from the north and provide a setting for the fulfillment of prophecies concerning the end time. Though scholars differ in their interpretations, a likely scenario is that Israel will be basking in the supposed safety of a peace treaty during the first half of the last seven years preceding the second coming of Christ. Though Israel is not at peace today, the coming world ruler is destined to give Israel her longed-for peace at the beginning of his political career. Anyone desiring to know God's program for the end time will be interested in what the Bible predicts concerning Russia. This book will challenge the student and enlighten the scholar.

JOHN F. WALVOORD

Preface to the 1987 Edition

More than a decade has passed since we first published *The Coming Russian Invasion of Israel* in 1974. What a decade it has been in further preparation toward the war Ezekiel prophesied. Think of the events that have transpired:

> Middle East manipulation of the world economy through the embargo and then overproduction of oil
>
> The Iranian revolution (Shah ousted; Khomeini installed)
>
> The Ethiopian revolution (Selassie ousted; Communists installed)
>
> The Iranian hostage crisis
>
> Israeli bombing of Iraqi nuclear plant
>
> Israeli-Lebanese war (vast caches of Soviet arms found in PLO warehouses)
>
> Libyan and other notably Syrian-backed terrorism, Western military retaliation
>
> Russian invasion of Afghanistan, Soviet gateway to the Middle East

The key figures of Ezekiel's prophesied war keep moving inexorably toward their great moment of destiny, without knowing that the Bible predicted their postures millennia ago. The Soviet Union continues to supply the enemies of Israel such as Syria and the PLO with money and arms. Iran (Persia) is embroiled in a debilitating war with Iraq. Ethiopia has been transformed through revolution from one of Israel's best friends in Africa to one of her worst enemies. Libya, under the radical leadership of Colonel Qaddafi, has fomented terrorism against every form of "Zionism" in the world, and has only recently pulled back its claws in response to U.S. military retaliation. The near neighbors of Israel—Lebanon, Jordan, and Egypt—have been somewhat neutralized through war or treaty. Only Syria remains as a determined enemy among Israel's immediate neighbors. Now Syria is being isolated as a terrorist state by England and other Western powers. The Middle East, because of its vast reserves of oil, continues to dominate the world's economy.

What can we say about all these developments? Shall we ignore them prophetically and consider them interesting geopolitical movements and nothing else? Not if we believe the Bible!

God, the great revealer of the future to Ezekiel and the other prophets, is obviously allowing all these things to occur so that the predictions in His Word may come to pass. The coming Russian invasion of Israel and the subsequent War of Armageddon are not pleasant things to write about, and we take no pleasure in describing the prophetic cataclysms ahead. Our only consolation is that these events are indications that the rapture of the Church must be ever closer to fulfillment and that the glorious return of our Lord Jesus Christ to the earth to establish His long waited kingdom may be coming sooner than many think.

We commit this little volume into the hands of our Lord that He might continue to use it to bring many to the realization of the truthfulness of His Word and the greatness of His salvation.

Preface to the First Edition

The world today is like a bomb with a lighted fuse. Conditions everywhere indicate that it is only a matter of time before the bomb is ignited and a global upheaval takes place.

The Coming Russian Invasion of Israel is a warning of the approaching explosion. Like a man who sees flames enveloping a building and cries, "Fire!" the authors sound an alarm.

It will not be surprising, then, that many will regard the authors as alarmists. In a sense, of course, that is exactly what they are. But when there is a real danger (and there is), anyone in his right mind appreciates being warned.

In the pages of this book there is not one note of false alarm. The coming catastrophe outlined is real. It is based upon that which is declared by God Himself in His eternal Word.

Biblical prophecy sets forth the future of Russia with dramatic clarity. Her invasion of Israel at the end of this age is incisively predicted in the Bible as clearly as the regathering of the Jews and their establishment as a present-day nation in Palestine.

This treatise on prophecy, though popularly written, constitutes a reliable guide to what is going to happen in the world in the near future. It will benefit everyone who reads it. The Christian will be strengthened in his faith in God's Word. The non-Christian will see his need of Christ's salvation to prepare him to face impending world catastrophe.

MERRILL F. UNGER

Introduction

This book has been exceedingly difficult to write because the events the authors intended to "predict" kept virtually coming to pass during the writing.

The authors are not the prophets, of course, but Ezekiel and other Bible writers who foresaw the coming Russian invasion of Israel have become so timely that it is difficult to set down interpretations of their prophecies before the events actually happen.

When we began this project in the summer of 1972, the idea of Russia's invading Israel was a matter of the future, though many recognized it as a possibility. But in the fall of 1973, during the writing, the Yom Kippur War broke out in the Middle East, and the American military went on "Alert," apparently fearing a Russian invasion of the combat area.

When the authors speculated, in 1972, that the oil of the Middle East might become a vital issue of world affairs, we didn't dream we would be waiting in line for gasoline in Texas a year later!

This book is more than timely. We believe that it is a grim necessity to warn the world, believers and unbelievers alike, that the biblical messages about today's world affairs are relevant and imminent. The coming Russian invasion of Israel is not far off, and it will profoundly affect us all.

Since 1948, when Israel was revitalized, the Arab world, Europe, and the superpowers have all been engaged in an escalating confrontation about the Jewish state. Russia has emerged as the major enemy of Israel over that time. We believe, with

Ezekiel, that Russia's animosity will not be satisfied short of an invasion.

Although this particular development has surprised the world, it comes as no surprise at all to students of the Bible. For 2,600 years, the Russian invasion of Israel in the end times has been common knowledge to readers of Ezekiel.

As with our first book, *Satan in the Sanctuary,* we have taken a single issue of Bible prophecy and have attempted to illuminate it completely in the light of current events. This time we have had to constantly revise the manuscript to keep up with ongoing developments. We felt, at times, that we might be too late. This may yet prove to be true.

But if you have this book in your hands before the Russian invasion of Israel, please know that the alarms sounded here are real. Ezekiel and the other prophets have been right too many times for the world to ignore them any longer.

And this issue is serious. It is truly a matter of life and death.

As we watch the coming Russian invasion of Israel in preparation, we pray that many thousands of readers will put their trust in the true Author of prophecy, the Lord Jesus Christ, and that believers in Christ will redouble their efforts to proclaim the redeeming Word of God while there is still time.

Until the coming Russian invasion of Israel, "The truth shall make you free" (John 8:32).

T. S. McCall
Zola Levitt

1
The Russians Are Coming

Russia is going to attack Israel.

Had we said that a few years back, it would have seemed a perfectly impossible idea, the way things stood.

But the prophet Ezekiel said it 2,600 years ago.

Ezekiel 36 to 39, which we will examine in detail, is one of the Bible's "histories of the future." It chronicles, by means of symbolic visions given to the ancient prophet, the coming Russo-Israeli war. It discusses the actual battle campaigns and the outcome, as seen by the war correspondent Ezekiel.

This event is not to be confused with Armageddon, the "war to end all wars." The Bible also foresees that ultimate conflict, but the Russo-Israeli war is to precede it.

Ezekiel places his prophecy in the end times. The Bible repeatedly refers to this final period of earthly history when God's plan for our world will culminate. It will not be a happy time. It is commonly called the Great Tribulation. And it seems to be coming up very soon.

Biblical descriptions of the end times include a host of issues quite familiar to readers of today's newspapers. Jesus, whose second coming is to climax the Tribulation period, warned His disciples about the strife and tension, false prophets, famines, earthquakes, and national conflicts that have now become the world's daily bread. He said, "Nation shall rise against nation," and He told of "wars and rumors of wars" (Matthew 24).

There is not adequate space here to consider all the prophecies about the end times and apply them to our world situation.[1] Suffice it to say here that the world today has all the requirements to satisfy Ezekiel's gruesome visions of the Russo-Israeli war and mankind's most comprehensive achievement of self-destruction, Armageddon.

Past ages could not hold a candle to us for weaponry, attitude, and the general know-how of destroying one another. The world has always had war, but our thermonuclear capabilities, international tension, and disregard for human life make us the best contenders ever for the honor of receiving the One who said sadly, "Except that the Lord had shortened those days, no flesh should be saved" (Mark 13:20).

If there is to be global war, we are the ones who can do it.

But first, the Russians are coming.

Ezekiel sees a massive land invasion from the far north into the Middle East. The Scriptures urge upon us that Russia will be the nation to mobilize an enormous land army that will cross the Caucasus Mountains, Turkey, Syria, and Lebanon to attack Israel. It's David and Goliath again, and again a question of the faithful against the pagans.

And again God takes quite an interest in the affair and sides with the underdog.

The outcome of the war is given: Russia meets her Waterloo. " 'I am against you, O Gog,' says God. 'You shall fall on the mountains of Israel, you and all your troops, and the people who are with you; I shall give you as food to every kind of predatory bird and beast of the field. You will fall on the open field; for it is I who have spoken,' declares the Lord God" (Ezekiel 39:1, 4-5).

The concept of a huge land army vanquished upon the open field is still very much a part of our modern warfare, automated as it is. We are going to discuss Russia's rationale for a march to Israel and the unique circumstances that will come about to satisfy the prophecy.

---

1. Hal Lindsey, *The Late Great Planet Earth* (Grand Rapids: Zondervan, 1970), and Thomas McCall and Zola Levitt, *Satan in the Sanctuary* (Chicago: Moody, 1973) give more complete discussions of end-time prophecies.

THE SICKLE AND THE SCIMITAR

For Ezekiel, to foresee an alliance between Russia and the Middle Eastern nations was going out on a limb. The pagan Middle East was, in his time, a most advanced civilization, the world's center of scientific knowledge and refinement of culture. It had dominated the Mediterranean for a period longer than from Christ to the present. Its magnificent architecture, religions, and military might were acknowledged and respected throughout the civilized world. But Russia, so far as anybody knew, was inhabited by roving bands of virtual cave people.

But look at the way things are now. Russia is a tremendous power. The claws of the bear have reached out in all directions from that vast frozen land, and Ezekiel is getting more believable by the day.[2]

The Arabs have become mere middlemen now as Russia advances upon the true cradle of civilization, the Holy Land.

In late October 1973 the American military went on "Alert" in an announced response to Russian troop movements. It was said that Russia was planning to move combat troops into the theaters of the Yom Kippur War. Some said the maneuver was purely a political gambit, but the important thing was that nobody was really surprised. For Russia to attack Israel would not be at all out of line with current developments.

That's never been true before. Until the present day, nobody except Ezekiel ever thought that Russia would attack the Holy Land.

But in the past twenty-five years [as of 1974—Ed.], Russia has increasingly become Israel's arch-enemy. She has armed the Arabs. There has been an enormous outlay of men and material for war steadily flowing to the Arabs from the Soviets, amounting to one of the most fearsome military mobilizations in history. Along with the death machines come talented Russian technicians to teach modern vengeance to the Arabs, who have no lack of vengeance in their own right.

2. For further information, see *Russia, Imperial Power in the Middle East* (Jerusalem: Carta, 1971).

THE YOM KIPPUR WAR, 1973
How close to a direct invasion of Israel by Russia?

Some of those Arab soldiers put on their first pair of boots one week and learn to use a rocket launcher the next. But the knowledge and the equipment keep piling up.

ISRAEL SEES RED

Israel does not regard the Arabs as the real enemy, wisely enough. When you're shot with a Russian-made AK 47, you might as well give credit where it is due.

General Moshe Dayan, hero of the 1967 Six-Day War, has stated flatly, "Israel is now at war with Russia."

The Arabs have their much-touted reasons to fight—they claim that the Jews took their land, they don't belong there, and so on. But the real issue here is Communism, the irresistible force of world atheism, against Judaism, the cradle of belief in God.

That is how Ezekiel saw things. Through him God named the real combatants—the enemies of God versus the friends of God.

2

The 4,000-Year Tragedy: Ezekiel the Prophet

The crowds must have really come out when Ezekiel held forth. His was a rare kind of ministry. He was a walking, talking example of national tragedy, demonstrating by his own sufferings what was to befall the nation of Israel. God told the Jews, "Thus Ezekiel will be a sign to you; according to all that he has done you will do" (Ezekiel 24:24).

It was a tough assignment. Patient Ezekiel, thought by some to be insane, endured an unrelenting series of personal tragedies and afflictions. He was a one-man show—a living drama of disaster.[1]

He shut himself up in his home, bound himself, and was struck dumb. He was ordered by the Lord to lie on his right side for 390 days and then on his left side for 40 more days, by way of demonstrating to Israel the number of years of her iniquity.

His food and water were rationed by God, and he was charged to eat disgustingly unclean bread, "having baked it in their sight over human dung" (4:12). He lost his wife but was not permitted even the consolation of mourning.

And that wasn't the half of it.

His suffering still goes on, in a way, because his majestic book is probably the least known and least heeded of the Bible prophecy books. With all of his painful efforts, his messages seemed largely lost on the ancient Jews and on us too.

It's time to give this unsung hero his due. We're about to see the fulfillment of his boldest, most dramatic visions reenacted

1. See Charles Lee Feinberg, *The Prophecy of Ezekiel* (Chicago: Moody, 1969), p. 224.

by whole nations rather than by one lone man of God.

He was one of the prophets of the Exile, the period when the majority of the Jewish nation was detained in Babylon in the sixth century B.C. King Nebuchadnezzar of Babylon had taken his place somewhere in the middle of the list of those tyrants of history with solutions to "the Jewish problem." He had laid siege to Jerusalem, examined his prisoners—an entire civilized nation—and simply carried off all but the poor and indigent.

In the bargain, he acquired some of God's key men. Ezekiel and the brilliant Daniel were among the captives. Jeremiah, whose clear-eyed forecast of this very disaster proved accurate to the letter, was left behind with those not worth deporting.

We can gather that the Jews were permitted to function within their traditions while detained, since the prophets went about their work. From the confines of ancient Babylon, Daniel and Ezekiel were able to see events of our own times and beyond. It is fair to say that they were able to see the end of the world as we know it.

Ezekiel's visions confounded his audiences, and they still leave the casual reader mystified. But as world events progress, we have the advantage of seeing the pieces fall into place. It would have been a lot to ask of the unhappy prisoners of Nebuchadnezzar to picture a mighty Russian army swarming down on Israel. But this is not nearly so hard to picture nowadays. Ezekiel is rapidly coming into fashion.

He begins his story of what we are calling the Russo-Israeli War with a typically bewildering vision of a valley filled with dried bones. God takes Ezekiel into this grisly scene to make a point. The prophet describes his conversation with God:

> And He said to me, "Son of man, can these bones live?" And I answered, "O Lord GOD, thou knowest." (37:3)

You can't blame him for hedging. Ezekiel must have been as baffled as we are.

God ordered Ezekiel to speak to the bones—to say to them, "O dry bones, hear the word of the LORD" (v. 4).

Some preachers today complain about speaking to "dead" audiences!

Ezekiel did as he was told, prophesying to the dead bones that they would live, that God would restore them with new sinews, flesh, skin, and breath.

The situation has been immortalized in the spiritual "Dry Bones." "Dem bones gonna walk aroun'," says the likable tune accurately enough. Ezekiel reports, "So I prophesied as He commanded me, and the breath came into them, and they came to life, and stood up on their feet, an exceedingly great army" (v. 10).

The meaning of the vision is revealed by God in the ensuing passages:

> Then He said unto me, "Son of man, these bones are the whole house of Israel: behold, they say, 'Our bones are dried up, and our hope has perished. . . .' Therefore, prophesy, and say to them, "Thus says the Lord GOD; 'Behold I will open up your graves and cause you to come up out of your graves, My people; and I will bring you into the land of Israel. (vv. 11-12)

The vision teaches the regathering of the Jews back to Israel from the "graveyards" of the Gentile nations.

This part of the prophecy is easy enough to understand for anyone living after A.D. 1948 when the Jews truly were regathered to their promised land. It wasn't quite as easy to appreciate for those living in the long nineteen centuries between the destruction of the second Temple of Jerusalem (A.D. 70) and 1948, during which time the Jews were dispersed and without a homeland.

To put Ezekiel and the end times into perspective, we should say something about the four-thousand-year tragedy that is the history of the Jews.

The Jews have had a special destiny since the day God made His covenant with Abraham (Genesis 12). They became for all time the chosen people. This status, though ultimately a profound blessing and privilege, has had its ups and downs. Be-

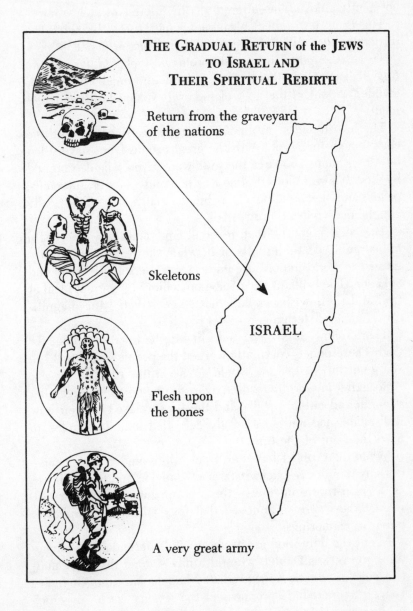

THE GRADUAL RETURN of the JEWS
TO ISRAEL AND
THEIR SPIRITUAL REBIRTH

Return from the graveyard
of the nations

Skeletons

Flesh upon
the bones

ISRAEL

A very great army

cause of the Jews' very special responsibility to God, they have constantly enjoyed, or suffered, divine interest in their affairs.

This is not just a theological viewpoint. History bears out the distinctive joys and deep despairs of this chosen people.

Tevye, the poignant Jewish protagonist of *Fiddler on the Roof*, cajoles God, "Why don't You choose somebody else for awhile?" A look at the story of Judaism explains his discouragement.

The Jewish nation, as a political entity, really began with the enslavement in Egypt. With the great exodus from slavery led by Moses about 1500 B.C., the Jews were given a land promised by God. There followed almost a thousand years of autonomy, peace, and the building of an intellectually and scientifically enlightened civilization in Israel.

The high point of that reverent and politically successful millennium was the middle of it, when the Jewish nation progressed to world importance under the leadership of David and Solomon. The brilliant King Solomon achieved the great ideal of God and the Jewish people when he constructed the magnificent Temple of Jerusalem.

There followed, however, a decline in the Jews' reverence for God. The prophets constantly warned the people—God had full charge of this nation and would act according to its faith.

Speaking in worldly terms, pagans to the north were gaining strength and military skills, and the Jews, relaxed in their now well-established and successfully defended kingdom, failed to heed the signs of the times.

When the prophet Jeremiah frantically sounded the alarm—actually naming Nebuchadnezzar of Babylon and the Chaldees as the near-future invaders—the government was unimpressed. In fact they were so annoyed that they jailed the prophet to quiet his clamorings.

About the only individual who thought Jeremiah had something to say was Daniel, who faithfully studied the older master's conclusions about the predicted Babylonian exile. God gave Daniel the incredible prophecy of the seventy weeks, in which he foresaw the advents of the reclaiming of Israel, the first coming of the Messiah, our own times, and even the future return of Christ.

Ezekiel was at this time carrying out his own difficult assignment among the captives and looking ahead to the far-future Russo-Israeli war.

The Jews were released from Babylon by the conquering Cyrus of Persia, as prophesied by Isaiah and Jeremiah, and once again they put their amazing nation-building powers to work.

By 516 B.C., they had established the second Temple in Jerusalem, and they proceeded though a shaky five centuries as a passive little country coexisting with Persia, Greece, and Rome.

They held on while Alexander the Great and numberless other pagan conquerors traded the known world back and forth, until the times of the Roman Empire.

Rome had a Russia-like knack of gathering territory, either quietly or with the sword, and a bottomless appetite for taxes. By the time of Christ, the Jews were exceedingly uncomfortable with their divided loyalties—their faith went to God, but their worldly produce went to Rome. They plotted rebellion.

This was a very bad idea. In a worldly way, they had no chance whatsoever in a war against Rome; spiritually they were in a state of extreme disobedience to God—they had rejected their Messiah.

They got together a national rebellion just after the time of Christ, in A.D. 66, and Rome dealt with it unmercifully. In the final siege of Jerusalem and the battle for the Temple site, the Jews suffered more than a million casualties in five months.

Only Hitler could rival such easy accumulation of Jewish bodies. The Jewish nation took more losses in that final campaign than the United States has suffered in all of her wars since 1776.

But the most unkind cut of all was the destruction of the second Temple. The Romans were so thorough that Jesus' prophecy was completely fulfilled; not one stone was left upon another.

But the depleted little nation staggered on. It's very hard to picture what a society is like when one out of every three people formerly functioning is dead. But the Jews somehow pulled their society back together and went on, heavily taxed and strictly policed by their Roman masters.

By the time of the emperor Hadrian, about A.D. 130, they were thinking rebellion again. There had been several skirmishes through the years, with heavy Jewish losses, and war on a national scale was in the offing. Hadrian provoked the Jews by building a pagan temple on the Jerusalem Temple site and forbidding or restricting many of the Jewish religious practices. He gave the Jews credit for Christianity—a charge they hardly appreciated. He was clearly trying to obliterate the very idea of Judaism, and he almost succeeded.

This war in A.D. 135 was actually a guerrilla operation in which the Jews fought like the Viet Cong; they spread the rebellion out over the whole of the country, picking at the Romans with endless small campaigns and ambushes. The enemy obliged with a nationwide mop-up.

The Jews were plainly too difficult to rule; the tedium of constant policing, the recurring combat, and the detested monotheism steadily emanating from Jerusalem finally tired the Romans, and they threw the Jews out of the land.

Thus began the great dispersion of the Jews that lasted until 1948.

There are no times of joy to report from that long period. Somehow the Jews, still faithful to their religious practices wherever they happened to be, never got themselves back together. From the days of Christ on, the Jews have had steady heartbreak.

The whole world now became the enemy of Judaism. Somehow no one could let the vanquished Jews just rest. They were slaughtered like animals during the Inquisition. They were starved and murdered endlessly in forced conversions throughout Europe. Persecution followed them to the ends of the earth.

Russia was no exception. The Jews suffered terrible pogroms and conversion-by-starvation. The present Soviet restrictions on Jewish emigration continue the tradition.

And finally Hitler came forward to attempt the complete extermination of the Jews.

This, at last, gave the world a bad conscience about the chosen people, and they were once again permitted their promised land.

The events since 1948 are within memory and show little slackening of the typical troubles for the Jews. The Arabs are following in the footsteps of the cruel Egyptians of antiquity; the Russians are getting up steam as Babylon did.

Now we turn to prophecy to know the future of Israel. Ezekiel will take us on from here.

From surveying Jewish history, we can better appreciate how much meaning there is in this "dry bones" vision of Ezekiel. "Can these bones live?" Can a people dispersed without a common culture for all those centuries ever pull themselves together again? Can dead things come back out of graves and be restored to their ancient land?

Only by an act of God.

"Then you will know that I am the LORD, when I have opened your graves and caused you to come up out of your graves, My people. And I will put My Spirit within you, and you will come to life, and I will place you on your own land. Then you will know that I, the LORD, have spoken and done it," declares the LORD. (37:13-14)

3
Brinkmanship:
Ezekiel the Political Analyst

Here comes the part we were telling you about.

Ezekiel now analyzes the coming Russian invasion of Israel. Chapter 38 introduces "Gog of the land of Magog, the prince of Rosh, Meshech, and Tubal" (v. 2), and says of them, "And you will go up, you will come like a storm, you will be like a cloud covering the land, you and all your troops, and many peoples with you. . . . And you will come from your place out of the remote parts of the north . . . a mighty army" (vv. 9, 15).

The names "Gog" and "Magog" are a bit cryptic, but it is not difficult to trace just who is meant here. Serious students of the Bible had identified Russia with these names long before she achieved her present supremacy.

The *New Scofield Reference Bible* states, "The reference is to the powers in the north of Europe, headed by Russia . . . the attempt to exterminate the remnant of Israel in Jerusalem."[1]

It is fascinating to compare the note to this passage found in the old Scofield Bible, annotated in 1909 during the Czarist age of Russia. The brilliant commentator C. I. Scofield could not have foreseen either the rise of Russia to world importance or the regathering of the Jews to Israel in 1948, but he says, "That the primary reference is to the northern (European) powers, headed up by Russia, all agree. . . . The reference to Meshech and Tubal (Moscow and Tobolsk) is a clear mark of identification. Russia and the northern powers have been the latest perse-

---

1. *New Scofield Reference Bible* (New York: Oxford, 1967), pp. 881-82 n.

cutors of dispersed Israel."[2] Scofield's reasoning has been kept
intact in the latest edition, with only the deletion of the word
"dispersed."

The genealogy of biblical names is a study in itself, and
beyond our scope here. *The Late Great Planet Earth* gives a
clear background in the chapter "Russia Is a Gog," pointing out
that the terms of Ezekiel 38 first appear in Genesis 10.[3] They
are actually names of sons and descendants of Noah, and it was
the custom for tribal, and finally national, names to evolve from
original founders' names. Apparently the tribal name Magog
moved northward from the Middle East. Josephus, a Romanized
Jewish historian of the first century, notes that Magog is called
the Scythians by the Greeks. Secular history books trace the
fierce Scythian people, who lived in the northern regions above
the Caucasus Mountains, as forerunners of modern Russia.

But even without all of that, we can still clearly see the Bear
of Russia through the geographical hints given by Ezekiel. He
stresses three times over that this mighty enemy of Israel comes
from the "uttermost north" (38:6, 15; 39:2; KJV*). The Hebrew
gives the qualifier meaning "extreme" or "uttermost" to the
term "north" all three times. And of course, the ultimate power
to Israel's uttermost north is Russia, the nation most likely to
succeed in being "a cloud to cover the land."

Furthermore, we have "Gog" identified as the "chief prince"
of the invaders. The Hebrew phrase translated "chief prince" is
nesi rosh. The word *rosh* can be an adjective meaning "head" or
"first," but it could just as easily be a place name "Rosh." The
Hebrew lexicon of Brown, Driver, and Briggs indicates that
Rosh here is the proper name of a people.[4] It seems that Ezekiel's Rosh has become today's Russia. This is more than a hint.
God indeed stands at the door and knocks.

And lastly, we have Meshech and Tubal, compared by Sco-

---

*King James Version.
2. *Scofield Reference Bible* (New York: Oxford, 1909), p. 883 n., Scofield's parens.
3. Hal Lindsey, *The Late Great Planet Earth* (Grand Rapids: Zondervan, 1970), p. 63.
4. Francis Brown, S. R. Driver, and Charles A. Briggs, *A Hebrew and English Lexicon of the Old Testament* (Oxford: Clarendon, 1959), p. 912.

field and many others to Moscow and Tobolsk, militarily indus-
trialized citadels of the future enemy. Moscow, as a matter of
fact, lies due north of Jerusalem.

Russia by herself would be sufficient as an enemy, or, as the
Jews sing on Passover, "*Dayenu!*" (enough for us). But Ezekiel
specifies that there will be some allies as well.

Persia, Ethiopia, and Libya are given, clearly enough, and
also Gomer and Togarmah (38:5-6). The latter two pertain to
eastern Europe (Iron Curtain countries) and southern Russia,
respectively, as we shall see. The former names have come down
to us intact except for Persia, which is now Iran.

Curiously, Egypt is not mentioned among the antagonists.
Will something happen to Israel's perennial enemy before the
conflict? Will she not be important enough to merit listing
among the allies at that time? Will the name Libya automatical-
ly include Egypt by then?

Persia, or Iran, would make a first-rate ally for Russia in a
land invasion of Israel. Its location and terrain would greatly
facilitate troop movements. Given the large scale of the invasion
foreseen by Ezekiel, the mountain ranges separating Russia
from the Holy Land become a factor; and those in Iran are
more hospitable than those in Turkey.

The Elburz mountain range in Iran is not so extensive as the
Caucasus in Turkey. The rest of Iran is generally more accom-
modating than hilly Turkey, too. And the advancing Russians
could create something of a pincer effect if they arrived from
two directions against Israel.

Ethiopia may represent more than the country that bears its
name. Its ancestry is traced to Cush, a grandson of Noah (Genesis 10), whose descendants apparently migrated southward into
all parts of Africa. The Organization of African Unity, founded
in 1963 in Addis Ababa, was described by Ethiopian emperor
Haile Selassie as "a single African organization through which
Africa's single voice may be heard."[5]

Libya's role is becoming more of a typecasting every day. It is

5. "Decade of Destiny," *Time*, 11 June 1973, p. 44.

RUSSIA WITH ALLIES ATTACKS ISRAEL
Ezekiel 38-39

easy to see that this advancing Arab power would be most receptive to participating in hostilities against Israel. It has ever been a nation typical of the Arab mentality and way of life, and it is presently arming. Giving some idea of how Libya is pressuring Ethiopia to work against Israel, a 1973 *Time* magazine report of a recent summit meeting of the Organization of African Unity says,

> Potentially the most divisive was a demand by Libya's Muammar Gaddafi for an all-out condemnation of Israel, and a break in relations by every O.A.U. state. Ethiopia and 26 Black African countries maintain diplomatic ties with Israel; Lybia, the O.A.U.'s five other Arab members and seven Black African nations are violently anti-Israeli.[6]

Gomer "and all his bands" is a reference to the countries of the Soviet bloc in Eastern Europe. Northward migrators who settled along the Danube and Rhine rivers, Gomer's descendants are traced through the ancient Cimmerians back to Genesis 10.

Togarmah is a reference to the area of southern Russia or Armenia and adds an interesting note to the method of invasion. The area is the origin of the Cossacks and is well known for its fine horsemen and its cultivation of superior cavalry forces. Ezekiel pictures horses being used in this invasion (38:15), and this very issue has been used many times to try to invalidate the prophecy. After all, who's going to ride a horse into a mechanized twentieth-century battle?

These critics were silenced during the Korean War when the Red Chinese, no mean horsemen themselves, moved huge numbers of troops in mountainous terrain by this tried and true method. The invasion of Israel involves mountainous terrain.

In any case, these last two allies, Gomer and Togarmah, complete the picture of the invading force. Israel is virtually surrounded. The Mediterranean Sea is at the west of the Holy Land, and the invading allies will come from the north, south, and east.

6. Ibid.

It makes so neat a geopolitical picture of a logical coming invasion that it is almost too perfect. Perhaps we cheated a little, looking at the current scene and bending the prophecy to fit it?

Actually, the placement of the allies was researched and decided by Bible students long before the Iron Curtain takeover of Eastern Europe, before the independence of Israel, before the rise of Russian Communism, and even before the alliance of distant nations was considered militarily feasible.

The Hebrew lexicon of Wilhelm Gesenius, written in the early 1800s, gives an analysis from which we do not differ.[7] Imagine what the scoffers thought back then!

THE CURRENT SCENE

We should go around the protagonists once more with a view to what they are doing on the current scene. Students of Ezekiel have never had a better opportunity to appreciate his foresight, and time may be running out.

First, Israel. Ezekiel beautifully pictures modern Israel with a few pointed remarks. He talks about the inner mountains of Israel "which had been a continued waste" (38:8). True enough, until the present era, Israel's fruitful mountains were constantly desecrated by foreign occupiers. The Muslims dammed up the rivers of the lush Sharon Valley and made it a marshland in order to deter invasion. The forests of the little country, always dependable, were destroyed by occupying Turks, who unfeelingly cut down the magnificent cedars to build temporary structures.

The "land of milk and honey" was made almost into a desert. King Solomon maintained a building program that was the envy of the ancient world, with largely domestic materials. But when the Jews got back their land in 1948, they had to first plant trees and restore natural irrigation in order to have wood. "Plant a tree in Israel" was the worldwide plea of the Jews in the

---

7. William Gesenius, *A Hebrew and English Lexicon of the Old Testament*, trans. Edward Robinson (Boston: Crocker & Brewster, 1854).

1950s, as schoolchildren sent their dimes to the Holy Land to restore it.

But a few verses later, Ezekiel pictures an improved land:

> And you [Gog] will say, "I will go up against the land of unwalled villages. I will go against those who are at rest, that live securely. . . . To capture spoil and to seize plunder, to turn your hand against the waste places which are now inhabited, and against the people who are gathered from the nations, who have acquired cattle and goods, who live at the center of the world" . . . to carry away silver and gold, to take away cattle and goods, to capture great spoil. (38:11-13)

This was quite a mouthful in Ezekiel's time. Who had ever heard of a land of unwalled villages back then? A wall to those ancient reckoners was what we call national defense today. The image shows how futuristic was the thinking of the prophet. And then we see that the invader, when he gets to "the desolate places that are now inhabited," will fall upon a people "that are gathered out of the nations." That must also have sounded strange to Ezekiel's audience; the Jews were not nomads, to say the least. Since they had a promised land, emigration was virtually a sacrilege. True, they were detained in Babylon because of military invasion, but Israel was still Israel. For the Jews to leave their land was to turn their backs on God. How could the prophet even speak of Jews as being gathered out of other nations?

Only an Ezekiel or a Daniel or an Isaiah—those possessed with the secret information given by God—could begin to picture the extent of Israel's coming exile.

Finally, in his statements about what the invader will encounter, Ezekiel depicts a successful nation, where the people "have gotten cattle and goods," and where silver and gold are there for the capturing.

What do these things symbolize? What does Israel have today that Russia would want?

Well, first there is very real wealth in Israel. The country is small but enjoys a vigorous economy. The people have a

Japanese-like enthusiasm that continually makes something out of nothing.

Then there is wealth in terms of raw materials. Little oil has been found there, but the mineral deposits of the Dead Sea, persistently defying extraction, represent a great prize. There is a wealth of brains, too. Russia gobbled up tremendous amounts of scientific and industrial know-how when she took over in Eastern Europe, particularly in East Germany.

We must keep in mind that invasions are not what they once were. When, for example, Nebuchadnezzar or the Assyrians accomplished an invasion, it was hard to tell a country had been there when they started. The new look in takeovers is much more discreet. The invading country attempts to leave intact all that might be useful to it—factories, farms, universities, laboratories—and have it all functioning on the invader's behalf. Ideally, the invader would like to just run up his flag on the flagpoles and leave everything else as it is.

The Russians are masters here. Occasionally they have "used the teeth on a knot that would not yield to the tongue," but they have by and large taken over vast amounts of the world with great discretion. Eastern Europe still functions; it just works for the Reds now. Where ideology would not work, they have employed tanks, but in any case the countries and their people end up second-class Russians.

Israel is a fine target for this kind of thing. She's the prize of the Middle East.

And finally, perhaps most important, Israel has a prime location for the orderly spread of Communism.

It is said that three things are important in real estate—location, location, and location. This applies whether you are buying the real estate or stealing it. Israel's location is of prime importance to Russia.

Looking on the world globe, one can see that Communism has enjoyed a steady, organized expansion emanating from Russia. It has gone to the Pacific on the east, the Berlin wall on the west, and to the frontier of the ice on the north. To the southeast it has penetrated Indochina with some difficulty. To the south-west—Israel's direction—it has jumped over some territory and penetrated in Africa and the Middle East. Israel stands right in the jumped-over spot.

Israel represents an outpost of democracy standing directly in the way of the communist expansion. She would provide a most convenient base from which the Communists could operate in the Middle East and Africa. She has good access by land and sea to these areas. Her harbors and airfields are among the best. The liability of the long supply line that has frustrated invaders from Alexander to Napoleon to Hitler would be eliminated in this sector if Russia could control Israel.

Ultimately, the oil of the Middle East might go to the great power close enough to grab it. The oil embargo proved how effective an economic and political weapon oil can be.

We have seen Russia establish outposts and then proceed from them to control vast territories. The situations in the Balkan and Ural countries led ultimately to the takeover of Eastern Europe. Operations from North Korea and North Vietnam were more troublesome but cost the free world dearly to contain them.

A foothold in Israel for the Russians would obviously mean trouble for everybody else.

Ezekiel's view of the spoils available seems conservative in view of the present scene.

Looking at the allies of Russia in the coming conflict, we can see that Ezekiel's stage is not completely set as yet—at least not at this writing.

Iran is not officially aligned with Russia at the moment, though such an alliance in the future would not be surprising. Ethiopia is not aligned with Russia either [as of 1974—ED.].

Libya is another matter. Some time ago she acquired fifty Mirage fighter jets from France, and she has learned how to use them (by trial and error). She has become an influential power with Egypt; indeed she may well supersede Egypt by the time of the invasion. Talk of a merger between the two nations is constant.

Libya's increasing importance in the Arab bloc, along with the fading of Egypt, may account for the lack of mention of

Egypt in the prophecy. There has been a shift recently to Libyan predominance in that sector. While Ezekiel's listeners could have easily understood the participation of Egypt in an invasion of Israel, he omitted her and mentioned Libya. Will Egypt decrease as a major power among the Arabs by the time of the invasion? Will Libya be the key antagonist from that sector?

The northern allies are already dressed for their roles. Gomer (Eastern Europe) can certainly be counted on by Russia to act on cue. Togarmah is literally part of Russia and may justify Ezekiel's unique picture of a horse-soldier invasion.

When will the invasion come?

We cannot know, even with today's insights, the times and seasons of the Father, taught Jesus, but we can watch the signs of the times and interpret them. We mentioned some of the signs of our times that qualify this present generation to be the one living in the end times, or "the latter days." This term, utilized by Ezekiel in this prophecy (38:8, 16; KJV), was also used by Jesus in His message about wars and rumors of wars. It is fair to say that all of our various circumstances might repeat together in some future time. But we would be remiss not to recognize the high correlation between the prophecy of Ezekiel and others and the characteristics of our age.

Historically, few people ever really took the prophets seriously. This was a very bad habit we should now break. With the restoration of Israel and the rise to world importance of Russia, Ezekiel's once-confusing messages take on a new urgency.

We have looked at the details of the Russian alliance and the present scene. Before we go on, we might do well to briefly review relations between Russia, the Arabs, and Israel. Are these nations really setting up for a major conflict at this time? Could Ezekiel have meant our generation? What about God's view? Israel is His chosen people.

In God's view, taught Ezekiel, this coming conflict is really a war between the atheists and the godly. The Arabs, sons of Ishmael and Muhammad, are virtually godless in the biblical view, while the Russians are outspokenly atheistic. The Jews, however far from their Messiah, are the worshipers of God in this conflict and will be able to count on His promises, in the prophet's view.

During the last twenty-five years [as of 1974—ED.] we have seen an evergrowing antagonism between the citadels of atheism and the Promised Land. When Israel was restored to the Jews, it brought up a feud that goes back four thousand years to the dispute between Isaac and Ishmael. The divine blessings and vast real estate holdings of their father, Abraham, were in question then.

They still are.

For nineteen centuries things were quiet between Jews and Arabs, while the Jews were dispersed throughout the world and the Arabs came and went as they pleased in Palestine. But Semites have long memories. When the Jews returned twenty-five years ago, they considered that they were getting back their land—the land promised to them by God.

The Arabs considered Israel (Palestine) to be their own ancestrally given property.

They might have worked something out, but Russia, hovering over the argument like a spectator at a prize fight, preferred the hostile atmosphere.

For her part, Russia at first thought Israel might be some sort of socialistic outpost in the Middle East, and she recognized the new state diplomatically in 1948. The original Israeli leaders, veterans of the kibbutzim—which resemble the Russian collective farms in some ways—seemed to embrace certain socialist concepts. But it was quickly seen by Russia that the new country was to be nothing like the materialistic, atheistic homeland of Communism.

The honeymoon ended very soon. Israel set up a kind of socialism that allowed for enormous concern for the individual human life, strong ties with theistic convictions and the Jewish heritage, capitalistic enterprise, and great political diversity. This was obnoxious to Russia.

Fissures appeared steadily in the relations between the two countries, until it was clear that the Russians preferred the company of the Arabs in the Middle East.

Three actual wars occurred—in 1956, 1967, and 1973—with Russia fully allied with the Arabs. Some propaganda about Russia's helping the Arabs recover their cherished land was published each time, but the pretenses have cleared up now. It's now plainly a matter of land-grabbing and the spread of Communism.

The wars helped show Russia and the world that the new little nation was no patsy. The Jews were reminded of the great days of King David, when invading armies confronted Israel only at their extreme peril. The war of 1967 demonstrated Israel as a power to be reckoned with. The world looked on in astonishment as the Jews vanquished the Russian-armed Arabs in just six days.

There is now relentless rhetoric about renewed hostilities, and fickle Russia still waits on the sidelines, armed to the teeth and making alliances. It appears she's just picking her moment.

These last twenty-five years [as of 1974—ED.] argue forcefully for Ezekiel's predictions coming to pass very soon. He gave no inkling of a lengthy period of brinkmanship but gave his analysis of the invasion in quick chronological sequence after the restoring of the Jews to their land.

Due to the strange dramatic manifestations of God's Word by the prophet, some people thought he was crazy. But he does not look crazy now.

Look now with Ezekiel at the actual Russian invasion of Israel.

4

From Russia with Blood: The Invasion of Israel

EZEKIEL: WAR CORRESPONDENT

"I am against you, O Gog," says the Lord at the beginning of Ezekiel 39. "I will turn thee back and leave but the sixth part of thee" (KJV).

In this stirring section, the prophet depicts in vivid detail the defeat of the mighty invader of the north and the terrible results of the war. "The sixth part" seems to refer to those spared of the vanquished Russian land force; this 84 percent casualty rate is unheard of in modern warfare.

It is hard to understand this severe defeat except as an act of God, which is what Ezekiel says it is. It accomplishes the purposes of glorifying God before Israel and the world and of finally restoring much-chastened Israel to its God.

Interesting details of the combat and its aftermath are revealed in this chapter. Some have raised controversies of interpretation, but the overall picture is distressingly clear.

Apparently Russia is overwhelmed early in her campaign, virtually at the moment of the invasion. We see no lengthy scenes of battle, and the attackers will "fall on the mountains" and "fall on the open field." The invasion does not appear to affect population centers, and we hear of no destruction of Israel (39:4-5). Shades of the Six-Day War!

We are given only a hint of this supernatural conquering of a militarily superior force. Ezekiel quotes God: "I shall strike your bow from your left hand, and dash down your arrows from your right hand. . . . And I shall send fire upon Magog" (vv. 3, 6). The

allies of the invader are disposed of as well! "You [Gog] shall fall
. . . and all your troops, and the people who are with you" (v. 4).

Fire falling upon a land army is not nearly as difficult to
imagine in this age as it was in Ezekiel's time. Napalm or even
nuclear detonations might well be described in this way. But this
is a matter of speculation. In the preceding chapter, Ezekiel
supplies more details, quoting the Lord: "I shall rain on him
[Gog], and on his troops, and on the many peoples who are with
him, a torrential rain, with hailstones, fire, and brimstone"
(38:22).

John F. Walvoord says, "Some natural questions are raised
about this. Some have suggested that the description of hailstones, fire and brimstone might be Ezekiel's way of describing
modern warfare, such as atomic warfare. There is a possibility
that Ezekiel was using terms he knew to describe a future
situation for which he did not have a vocabulary. The language
of Scripture indicates, however, that the victory over this invading horde is something that God does. It is God, Himself, who is
destroying the army."[1]

Ezekiel goes into quite a bit of detail about the aftermath of
the war. Enough is left for scavenging birds and animals; "I shall
give you as food to every kind of predatory bird and beast of
the field" (39:4). The dead bodies of the invaders apparently
will strew the fields and mountains of the holy land: "For seven
months the house of Israel will be burying them in order to
cleanse the land" (v. 12).

This lengthy burial detail will occupy a lot of people: "Even
all the people of the land will bury them" (v. 13), and some will
find full-time employment at it: "And they will set apart men
who will constantly pass through the land burying . . . those left
on the surface of the ground, in order to cleanse it" (v. 14).

With typical Israeli civic pride and endeavor, they will steril-
ize their promised land. Even travelers through the land—tour-
ists—are to be asked to watch for stray remains and to mark the

---

1. John F. Walvoord, *The Nations in Prophecy* (Grand Rapids: Zondervan, 1967), p.
113.

spot for the burial details: "And as those who pass through the land pass through and anyone sees a man's bone, then he will set up a marker by it until the buriers have buried it in the valley of Hamon-gog" (v. 15). "Hamon-gog" is the Hebrew for "The multitude of Gog," which is to become the name of this vast cemetery for the invaders.

This grim and morbid information about the burial emphasizes the very large size of the invading force and the totality of its defeat. But even more of a testimony to this will be the burning of the weapons that fall from the hands of the combatants. Ezekiel specifies that seven years will be involved in the burning of the weapons of this vast army.

"Then those who inhabit the cities of Israel will go out, and make fires with the weapons and burn them . . . and for seven years they will make fires of them" (v. 9). This has a practical side: " 'And they will not take wood from the field or gather firewood from the forests, for they will make fires with the weapons; and they will take the spoil of those who despoiled them, and seize the plunder of those who plundered them,' declares the Lord GOD" (v. 10).

So the trees of Israel, so lovingly planted one by one, are to be spared, while the weapons of the pillager are used for firewood. It all fits with the frugal, spartan ways of the native Israeli.

It fits, too, with the Israeli tradition of commemorating any struggle for the Holy Land. Today [1974—ED.] in Israel one sees 1948-model trucks and armored weapons—vehicles of every kind—still standing at the sites of their final battles. The Israelies leave them by the sides of the roads to remind the people how difficult this land was to attain. A French-built Renault tank stands in the brush at the southern tip of the Sea of Galilee, blasted into submission by a Molotov cocktail. It commemorates the successful defense of unarmed Daganya Kibbutz against a column of twenty-six Syrian tanks in the 1948 war of independence.

It would be fitting indeed for the Israelis to watch a seven-year memorial fire symbolizing still another defense of the Promised Land.

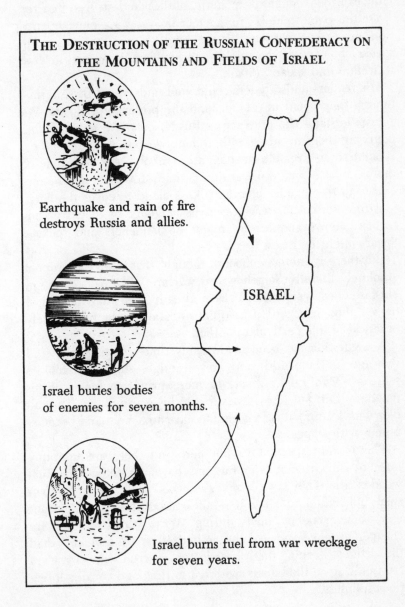

THE DESTRUCTION OF THE RUSSIAN CONFEDERACY ON THE MOUNTAINS AND FIELDS OF ISRAEL

Earthquake and rain of fire
destroys Russia and allies.

ISRAEL

Israel buries bodies
of enemies for seven months.

Israel burns fuel from war wreckage
for seven years.

But how can they burn tanks, trucks, and armored vehicles? How can the weapons of modern conflict be destroyed by fire?

On this point there is still much controversy. Ezekiel's descriptions are in keeping with his time and his own vocabulary. He speaks of burning "the shields and bucklers, bows and arrows, war clubs and spears" (39:9).

His readers and listeners could well understand these terms, though they could not understand the presence of Russia. We can understand the presence of Russia, but have some trouble picturing them invading with archaic weaponry.

Some think Ezekiel's weapons are symbolic representations of the weapons of modern warfare. Perhaps, for example, the reference to the invader coming "like a cloud to cover the land" (38:16) describes air warfare in the language of the sixth century B.C. Bows and arrows might be launchers and rockets. Spears might be rifles.

But there is another school of thought that takes the prophet absolutely literally. Somehow this warfare will revert to use of old-fashioned weapons. We have already seen that the use of horses, though regarded as quite archaic, might be uniquely practical in this particular conflict.

A suggestion has been made many times relating to the oil shortage in the world, and how it might stop all machines someday. Man might revert to more primitive means if his machines fail, but he will never stop his war-making. The soldier with a jammed rifle is glad to have a bayonet and becomes a man with a spear.

This is most speculatory, but here and there are tempting hints of such things. The Russians have perfected an actual wooden rifle. They have compressed wood until it is harder than steel, but lighter to carry. It is still combustible. The Germans used some wooden bullets during World War II; they were cheaper to make and had the desired effect. In fact, they had the virtue of keeping the Allies' doctors overrun with surgery in the fields, since the bullets shattered in flesh and became infectious splinters.

Up-to-date news about poachers shooting bears in the American national parks tells of the use of crossbows instead of rifles. Quieter, cheaper, just as accurate, and just as deadly!

It is difficult to imagine a modern nation fielding a land army outfitted with the ancient weapons, however. But, again, it has proved equally difficult to disagree with a biblical prophet.

Another idea is that the fire itself may be unconventional. Ordinarily fire burns wood, but nuclear fire burns metal. God's great fire from heaven that stops the invasion has been considered as a reference to thermonuclear phenomenon. Perhaps the Israelis will have the means to actually burn modern armored weaponry.

Still another speculation on this seven-year fire is acetylene, used in torches that cut, rather than burn, metal. It is still fire, and we do use it to destroy metal, such as in train-wreck rescues.

All these exercises, again, are mere speculation to try to uncover the meanings of Ezekiel's prophecies. But they serve the good purpose of demonstrating that prophecy is not to be summarily discarded because of its archaic language or ancient-seeming settings. Men have learned slowly but surely not to scoff at even the most "dated" terminology of Bible references. As the oft-quoted Ecclesiastes 1:9 puts it, "There is nothing new under the sun."

With the beginning of the seven-year fire, the Russo-Israeli war concludes. There is certainly no doubt of the victor. The aftermath of the war apparently exceeds all post-conflict carnages in man's long history of war. The scavenger beasts and birds are cheated of their foul prey only by full-time burial squads, with the participation of "all the people of the land" and travelers besides. Seven months to bury the dead, seven years to consume the residue of armaments in fire.

What is it all for? For the greater glory of God. Specifically, to testify of the power and the compassion of the Lord, and to explain at last the four-thousand-year tragedy of the chosen people.

For the benefit of the Gentiles, God has shown His glory:

And I shall set my glory among the nations; and all the nations will see My judgment which I have executed, and My hand which I have laid on them. (Ezekiel 39:21)

For the benefit of the Jews, God has staged this miraculous victory:

And the house of Israel will know that I am the LORD their God from that day onward. (v. 22)

And for the benefit of all, the lesson Ezekiel tried to teach is repeated:

The house of Israel went into exile for their iniquity because they acted treacherously against Me, and I hid My face from them; so I gave them into the hand of their adversaries, and all of them fell by the sword. (v. 23)

Indeed, all of the prophecies portrayed by Ezekiel's painful demonstrations—the mortification of the prophet before the people's eyes—came to pass just as God originally said they would:

According to their uncleanness and according to their transgressions I dealt with them, and I hid My face from them. (v. 24)

Chapter 39, the conclusion of this great prophecy which began with the dry bones vision and culminated in the Russo-Israeli war, has a happy ending for the Jews. They are to be reconciled to God:

When I bring them back from the people and gather them from the lands of their enemies, then I shall be sanctified through them in the sight of the many nations. Then they will know that I am the LORD their God because I made them go into exile among the nations, and then gathered them again to their own land; and I will leave none of them there any longer. (vv. 27-28)

The section ends with a wonderful promise by God that He will not chastise Israel again and that He has now made the ultimate effort to secure His people.

> "And I will not hide my face from them any longer, for I shall have poured out My Spirit on the house of Israel," declares the Lord God. (v. 29)

This final blessing has the characteristic of a messianic deliverance and has caused many interpreters to believe that the battle described earlier is actually the battle of Armageddon. Armageddon immediately precedes the advent of the millennial kingdom, which at last brings real peace.

This is possible, but we think that there are enough distinguishing characteristics between the Russian invasion and the war called Armageddon to consider them to be separate conflicts. We think, however, that the results of the Russian invasion lead directly to Armageddon.

In the next chapter we will discuss this war-to-truly-end-all-wars. No discussion of the affairs of mankind would be complete without Armageddon, the net result of man's efforts without God.

Apparently the demonstration of disaster that is the Russian invasion of Israel is insufficient to impress the world to seek salvation with God. "All the nations will see My judgment which I have executed" (v. 21), says the Lord, but somehow all the heathen get embroiled in Armageddon.

Men will see God in action but will still reject Him. There is nothing new under the sun.

5

Satan on the Battlefield:
The Armageddon

The Russian invasion of Israel, in all its horror and devastation, will be only a curtain raiser.

Men will achieve much more in the Armageddon. In this chapter we're going to talk about *war!*

This global catastrophe will involve the entire race of man. No nation will escape. It is within reason to expect a billion casualties. Jesus said that if He were to delay His return, during this conflict "no life would have been saved" (Matthew 24:22).

Our two world wars, and all that went before and since among the races and nations of mankind, will be regarded as so much petty quibbling compared to this grand finale. All of man's most sophisticated science and technology will be placed in the service of his most primal lusts. Power-maddened armies numbering in the hundreds of millions will fall upon the Holy Land and upon each other, and only the patient God of our creation will be able to stem the tide.

The Armageddon conflict grows out of the Russian invasion of Israel. There is a great deal of uncertainty on this particular prophetic point. That the Russian invasion will happen is clear, but just when and how it is juxtaposed with the other issues of the end times has raised some controversy.

The problem is the placement of the invasion itself. It precedes Armageddon, but it is not completely clear how *far* before it. Some hold it to be a part of Armageddon, and some have it very much before the great war. The accompanying chart shows that scholars have attempted to place the grisly work of Gog and Magog at almost every point along the future prophetic timetable.

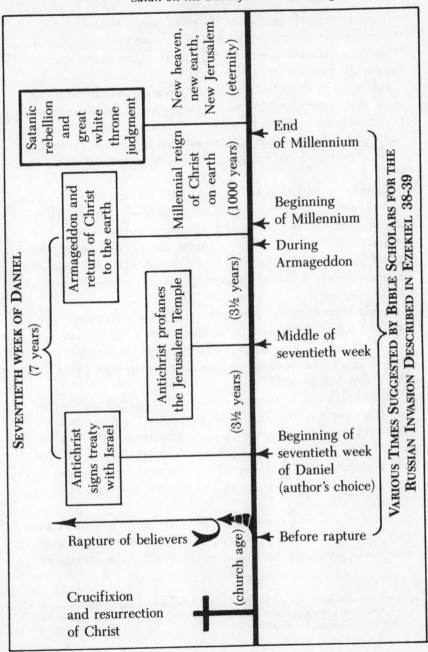

The problem of comparing different prophets and scheduling, as it were, their different foreseen events on a future timetable has its hazards. There are very good arguments for each of the positions shown on the chart.

It is our conviction that the Russian invasion of Israel will take place at a point very close to the beginning of the Tribulation period—Daniel's seventieth week. This is the moment when the Antichrist comes forward with his solution to the tensions in the Middle East and his infamous covenant with Israel (Daniel 9:27).

Daniel's seventieth week is calculated to last seven years, during which the great end-time prophecies will run their course until the second coming of Christ to the earth. The indication by Ezekiel (Daniel's contemporary) that Israel will spend seven years gathering up the debris from the Russian invasion to use for fuel is a tempting corollary to the seventieth week.

Could Daniel's seventieth week and Ezekiel's seven years refer to the same time period? We think this is highly plausible, and this is one of the reasons we suggest that the Russian invasion of Israel will occur somewhere near the beginning point of the Tribulation period.[1]

Possibly the annihilation of Russia as a military force will set the stage for the Antichrist's rise to power. He represents the revived Roman Empire, the ten-nation confederacy of Europe, and thus he would profit by the removal of this major rival for world domination. Israel would also be ripe for some peacemaker after the experience of the Russian invasion, even in victory.

Armageddon will come about through mismanagement by the Antichrist. He will first deliver on his promise to Israel; peace will prevail in the Holy Land for half of the Tribulation

---

1. For a complete analysis of the prophecy of the Tribulation period and the actions of the Antichrist in connection with it, see Thomas McCall and Zola Levitt, *Satan in the Sanctuary* (Chicago: Moody, 1973).

period—three and one-half years. During this time the Antichrist will set up an effective world domination, steadily gaining economic and political control over the nations. Everyone will buy and sell everything in accordance with the fiscal system of the Antichrist (Revelation 13:17), and even the very elect of God—the Jews—will be fooled by the calm before the storm.

Only in these days of computers and numerical designations like credit card numbers and social security can we fully appreciate a world financial system. It used to take some imagination to see how the Antichrist could ever pull this off, but in these days of common currency and common markets it seems quite natural. In fact, it will seem like a great improvement over the past.

And perhaps it will be, in some ways, but the Antichrist will not be able to control his lust for power. When his total socio-politico-economic system is functioning on a worldwide scale, he will decide that he needs a title.

He will proclaim himself God!

It takes a special kind of egomaniac to choose that highest of titles. The Antichrist will not mean that he is *like* God, or has the virtual *power* of God over men; he will declare that he *is* God!

In 2 Thessalonians 2:4 the apostle Paul pictures that one-of-a-kind blasphemy. "He takes his seat in the temple of God, displaying himself as being God."

The Antichrist will enter the Tribulation Temple, the third Jerusalem Temple, which will stand at this time, and plainly announce that he is God. Jesus specified that this "abomination of desolation," foreseen earlier by the prophet Daniel, would happen "in the holy place" of the Temple—the sacred sanctuary where God was said to dwell among His people (Matthew 24:15).

This incredible act clearly identifies the power behind the Antichrist. It is Satan's desire to replace God on earth; the Scriptures testify to this ongoing conflict since Satan's fall from heaven. The Antichrist will be Satan's most successful attempt to replace the Almighty. In the manner that God sent His Son to the earth, Satan will send the Antichrist, another resurrected "savior."

But the Jews have always regarded blasphemy as the highest of crimes, and they will recoil in horror from this action by their former mentor.

When Jesus identified Himself as the Son of God, there was much controversy among the Jews. The gospels tell of scenes of argument and whispered speculation about the remarkable Teacher of Galilee. The nation officially did not accept their Messiah, though enough Jews did that a church of Jerusalem was founded and the Word was promulgated to the world.

But this time—the Antichrist's time—there will be no such controversy. Israel will revolt.

From that moment on, the Antichrist's uneasy world peace will be shattered. The blasphemy occurs at the midpoint of the seven-year Tribulation period, so that three and one-half years are left to the mobilizations, invasions, and conflicts of the world armies leading up to the ultimate battle of Armageddon. The collision course is set when the Antichrist enters the Temple and proclaims himself God. He will become Satan on the battlefield.

Daniel chronicles an attack by kings of the north and south against the Antichrist in Israel. Apparently, once the fragile peace is ruined, men will at once resort to their former ways. Israel's revolt will show the Antichrist to be less than supernatural and may inspire widespread revolution against the dictator. Perhaps the attacking powers will consider the Antichrist's hold on things to be weakened by the Israeli revolt.

In any case, "the king of the South will collide with him, and the king of the North will storm against him with chariots, with horsemen, and with many ships," says Daniel (11:40). The Antichrist will have his hands full.

Many competent interpreters of prophecy have equated this king of the north with Ezekiel's Gog, who perpetrated the Russian invasion. This is one of the controversies existing about just when the Russian invasion occurs in the scheme of things. Naturally, if the king of the north is Gog, then the Russian invasion would occur after the Antichrist's blasphemy, or after the half-way point of the Tribulation period. The king of the north reacts to Israel's revolt.

But we are disinclined to equate these two invaders. Ezekiel's Gog comes from the "uttermost north," and Daniel's king of the north is discussed in connection with his prophecies about the Greco-Syrian powers. We have already seen that Russia fits best the description of Gog's land for many reasons. In considering the king of the north, we must take into account Daniel's context. Daniel discusses, in chronological order, the four powers of Bible history, and his king of the north comes up in connection with the third such power—the Greco-Syrian power. Daniel 11:40-45 describes a purely Middle Eastern conflict, closer to home than the allied powers that descend in the invasion of Ezekiel 38 and 39.

Thus we are persuaded that the Russian invasion is separate from, and previous to, the invasion of the king of the north. As we understand the scenario, it will be Syria, united with Egyptian powers (the king of the south), who will attack the Antichrist and Israel.

Again, we do not sound very revolutionary to suggest that someday Egypt and Syria will mount a simultaneous attack against Israel.

But let us give credit where it is due. Daniel said it twenty-six centuries ago!

The present Middle Eastern conflicts are not to be confused with these future prophetic events, of course, but we can certainly see the stage being set. What an advantage we have over commentators of the past who could not even see an Israeli nation (before 1948), let alone these alliances and invasions. If we live long enough, we will see all prophecy fulfilled.

This invasion by the kings of the north and south ignites the whole of the world. The Antichrist will call upon his Western forces, the ten-nation confederacy of Europe, and the kings of the East (probably the massive hordes of China) will join in.

That will be a dramatic moment! From what we can gather, a 200,000,000-man army will *march* to the scene of the conflict in Israel from the east (Revelaton 9:16).

The mighty Euphrates River, which would present an obstacle to a marching army from the east, will be dried up in the end times, according to prophecy. The Asian horde, nearly as large as the entire population of the United States, will wreak havoc on this terrible venture. They will account for the wiping out of a third of the earth's population (Revelation 9:18).

It all becomes very reasonable, if terrifying. Two hundred million soldiers was an unthinkable number at the time John wrote his astonishing book of Revelation, but China today would be able to field such an army. And uniquely, although China is the only power who could assemble such numbers, she is not equipped to transport them by mechanized means. If China seriously wanted to invade the Middle East, she would indeed be obliged to *walk* there. She does not have the ships and planes for transporting any sort of large army, let alone the behemoth foreseen by John.

So these are the combatants: the kings of the east, north, and south, and the European confederacy of the Antichrist. Israel will be stage-center as usual; she won't have to travel anywhere to participate in this war.

Russia will have already been neutralized by the stunning catastrophe of the earlier invasion of Israel. As for the other nations, the world is too small to escape the holocaust. The United States, not specifically mentioned in prophecy, will likely either be allied with the European confederacy (such as now in NATO) or be a helpless casualty of global thermonuclear effects. These are suggested by repeated descriptions of raining fire, brimstone, smoke, and so on found in connection with these final conflicts.

THE BATTLE OF ARMAGEDDON

It's not quite clear who fights with whom about what. Getting there, as we have seen, is half the war.

Armageddon is different from what we have experienced in the history of our wars, not just in its scope but in its quality of supernatural events. Utilizing the same source—the Bible—which gives all the events leading up to this battle (and all of the fulfilled prophecy of the past), we find a curious story replete with divine actions.

Zechariah covers the action of the war and gives in ominous tones the perennial hazards of making war on Jerusalem and Israel: "Behold, I am going to make Jerusalem a cup that causes reeling to all the people around; and when the siege is against Jerusalem, it will also be against Judah. And it will come about in that day that I will make Jerusalem a heavy stone for all the people; all who lift it will be severely injured. And all the nations of the earth will be gathered against it" (12:2-3).

All those who tangle with Jerusalem will be "cut in pieces" indeed. Despite the best efforts of the world's most capable and fanatic invaders through four thousand years of bloody conflict, Jerusalem has survived; and it will continue to survive.

The huge world forces come together where they have room to do their fearsome work—in the valley of Megiddo in quiet Galilee. In that valley, "called in the Hebrew tongue Armageddon" (Revelation 16:16), untold millions of soldiers armed with the ultimate weapons of war will stage mankind's most effective attempt at suicide. Blood will flow, according to Revelation, "up to the horses' bridles" (14:20).

Jerusalem, nearly one hundred miles away from the combat zone, will not be spared the effects of this horrifying conflict. Zechariah laments, "The city will be captured, the houses plundered, the women ravished, and half of the city exiled" (14:2). Considering the pure numbers of the invading forces, no portion of little Israel will be safe from actual combat. And Jerusalem, God's city, veteran of invasions, rapings, and lootings from time immemorial, will have to endure this one last catastrophe.

But in this final hour of terrible conflict, something miraculous will transpire among the people of Israel. Pressed to the wall, the Promised Land torn apart in vicious war, their historic fears of national annihilation coming to reality before their eyes, the Jews turn to God. They have always done this, but in this case they turn to their Messiah—at last! It seems that the testimony of the 144,000 Hebrew Christians, who minister on earth after the rapture and who share their faith in Christ, at last gets a hearing in Israel.

Jesus said clearly enough, "No one comes to the Father, but through Me" (John 14:6), and the Jews, in a time when their need to come to the Father is greater than ever before, will turn to their native Son, the carpenter of Nazareth. Jesus will be accepted as the true Messiah of Israel.

Isaiah 53, the conscience of the Jewish people, will be read with new understanding in Israel. "He was despised and forsaken. . . . And we did not esteem Him. We hid . . . our faces from him. . . . But He was pierced through for our transgressions, he was crushed for our iniquities" (vv. 3, 5). Whether out of the desperation of the tragic moment, or from the testimony of the Christian witnesses, or from a national realization that disaster has ever followed the Jews since the time of Christ, the Jewish nation will completely awake to Christ. They will finally say, "Blessed is the one who comes in the name of the Lord."

This is the password to salvation for the Jews. Jesus told them, while He was on the subject of the destruction of Jerusalem in His prophecy (Matthew 23:37-39), that He would not return until they welcomed Him in the words of Psalm 118:26: "Blessed is the one who comes in the name of the LORD."

It will be the greatest spiritual awakening in all of history, as the Jews come to Christ by the millions. It will be a true Day of Atonement in Israel: "In that day a fountain will be opened for the house of David and for the inhabitants of Jerusalem, for sin and for impurity (Zechariah 13:1). "And thus all Israel will be saved" (Romans 11:26).

God is practical. He promised deliverance to Israel when the nation was faithful. He demonstrated this in bringing His chosen out of Egypt in a miraculous deliverance in the time of Moses. He will do no less in the time of the Armageddon.

The Jews receive Christ in a moment, as it were. There is no time to build a lot of churches or to ponder a lot of Scripture

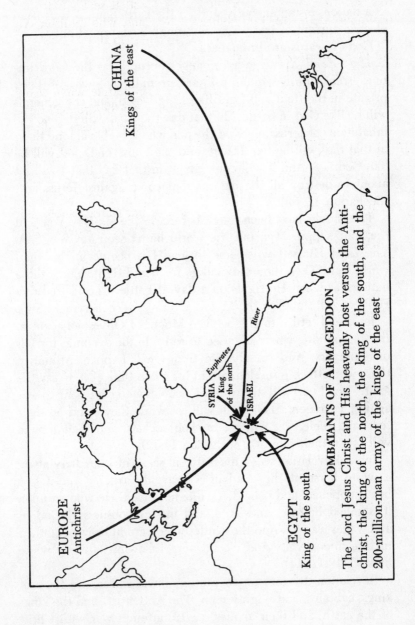

CHINA
Kings of the east

EUROPE
Antichrist

SYRIA
King of the north

Euphrates River

ISRAEL

EGYPT
King of the south

COMBATANTS OF ARMAGEDDON

The Lord Jesus Christ and His heavenly host versus the Antichrist, the king of the north, the king of the south, and the 200-million-man army of the kings of the east when Armageddon is going on in your land. The nation is saved as a nation, instantaneously, and on the battlefield. It is as if an electric current of truth is shot through everyone at once.

God's rewards are immediate.

The tide of Armageddon changes abruptly as the Lord imbues Israel with newfound military strength. The weakest buck private in the field will fight like King David, and the generals will be like God in battle: "In that day the LORD will defend the inhabitants of Jerusalem, and the one who is feeble among them in that day will be like David, and the house of David will be like God. . . . And it will come about in that day that I will set about to destroy all the nations that come against Jerusalem" (Zechariah 12:8-9).

The Israelis have been tough before, in the Six-Day War and the Yom Kippur War, but the world hasn't seen anything yet. The Lord Himself will come to lead His people in this final world war. "Then the LORD will go forth and fight against those nations, as when He fights on a day of battle. And in that day His feet will stand on the Mount of Olives" (Zechariah 14:3-4).

Jesus will return to His beloved Mount of Olives, adjacent to the Temple site, where He used to retire in the evenings for His own prayers. And cataclysmic things will happen. Militarily, those who attack Jerusalem are in for a bad time of it, to say the least. "The LORD will strike all the peoples who have gone to war against Jerusalem; their flesh will rot while they stand on their feet, and their eyes will rot in their sockets, and their tongue will rot in their mouth" (Zechariah 14:12).

John's Revelation sees a magnificent scene of Jesus arriving on a white horse at the head of a heavenly army: "And I saw heaven opened; and behold, a white horse, and He who sat upon it is called Faithful and True; and in righteousness He judges and wages war. . . . And the armies which are in heaven, clothed in fine linen, white and clean, were following Him on white horses" (19:11, 14).

Revelation 19 goes on to picture fowls eating the flesh of kings, captains, and mighty men. The Antichrist "and the kings of the earth, and their armies" (v. 19) attempt war with Christ and His heavenly troops, with predictable outcome. John sees no scenes of lengthy battle, and Revelation goes immediately to the disposal of the Antichrist and his schemes for world domination in the "lake of fire" (v. 20).

The troops of the Antichrist, who represent, of course, the enormous armies of the Gentile nations of the world, are "killed with the sword which came from the mouth of Him who sat upon the horse, and all the birds were filled with their flesh" (v. 21).

This supernatural ending to the battle of Armageddon is not new in biblical accounts. We may say that there are natural wars and supernatural wars in connection with Jewish history, which is the story of a people whose destiny is controlled by God. The deliverance of the Jews from Egypt showed the loss of the Egyptian forces when they tried to cross the Red Sea on the dry land used by the Jews.

David experienced a supernatural victory over Goliath in response to his faithfulness. Joshua demolished the walls of Jericho with trumpets. The Maccabees experienced the miraculous touch of God when they defeated Antiochus and rededicated the second Temple.

Armageddon follows suit, demonstrating that God responds to true faith. When the Gentile nations first march against the Holy Land, they certainly have no fear of the little Israeli army. They plunder Jerusalem and set up their bloodletting in Galilee, indifferent to the great people whose land they desecrate.

But what a different story when the Jews turn to Christ! How shocking for the Gentiles to suddenly face an army of King Davids with Jesus Christ at the head of it!

We have not experienced a supernatural war for some time. The Russian invasion of Israel, with its strange annihilation of the invading forces, is the first of this final period. On that occasion the issue is atheism versus faith in God, and as we have seen, God takes a hand in it. It is almost a smaller picture of the vicious Armageddon to follow.

Armageddon is the end of war. It marks the return of Jesus to the earth for an extended stay and a new kingdom. The great age of "peace on earth, good will toward men" is ushered in at the climax of Armageddon.

With this period of world cataclysm, begun with the Russian invasion of Israel and ended with Armageddon out of the way, let's look to happier times. Our discussion would not be complete without an encouraging look at the return of Jesus Christ.

6
"Thy Kingdom Come"

Jesus will not return strictly for His military mission. We can be thankful enough that the battle at Armageddon is stopped short of annihilating all mankind, but the Lord will return for a greater purpose. He will establish the first successful, peaceful, equitable world government. His will shall be "done in earth, as it is in heaven."

The inexorable series of cataclysmic events proceeding from the Russian invasion of Israel goes on, as Jesus occupies His throne of glory and confronts what is left of man's broken-down world.

How Did You Treat My Brothers?

First Jesus will judge the nations of the world—the Gentiles.

This will be quite a different Jesus from the sacrificial lamb of the gospels. The Savior, who endured humiliation, torture, and physical death at the hands of the unbelieving, will return as a Lion.

He had taught His followers to pray, "Thy kingdom come, Thy will be done, on earth as it is in heaven" (Matthew 6:9), and He will see to it that this prayer is answered at once.

Here is how things will stand as the Lord operates His office of immigration into the new kingdom: the Gentiles of the world, the survivors of Armageddon, will be judged; for two other groups the judgment process will be waived. One of these will be the unique group of past believers—those of Old Testament times and of the church age, along with those believers who died as martyrs in the Tribulation. They will be resplendent in their resurrection bodies. The remaining group will be the Christian nation of Israel.

As we have seen, all Israel will be redeemed at what looks to be its final hour. They will have carte blanche into the millennial kingdom, as will all other believers. As Paul exulted, "All Israel will be saved" (Romans 11:26).

And that takes care of everybody. The dividing line is Christ, who says, "If you are not *for* Me, you are *against* Me."

Israel will take its guaranteed place as "the head [of the nations] and not the tail" (see Deuteronomy 28:13). Jesus will judge and govern in Jerusalem, the new world capital in the Millennium. All the law of the world will emanate from Jerusalem as, in a way, it always did.

Now back to the Gentiles who will stand trial before Jesus. They will at least have a fair Judge, but the issue of whether they have believed or not will have really caught up with them this time.

Jesus will ask, "How did you treat My brothers?" The beautiful chapter Matthew 25 gives a transcript of that future courtroom scene:

> But when the Son of Man comes in His glory, and all the angels with Him, then He will sit on His glorious throne. And all the nations will be gathered before Him; and He will separate them from one another, as the shepherd separates the sheep from the goats; and He will put the sheep on His right, and the goats on the left. (vv. 31-33)

Nobody gets to testify because, by the Lord's criteria, all already have. After He separates the defendants into the two groups,

> then the King will say to those on His right, "Come, you who are blessed of My Father, inherit the kingdom prepared for you from the foundation of the world. For I was hungry, and you gave Me something to eat; I was thirsty, and you gave Me drink; I was a stranger, and you invited Me in: naked, and you clothed Me; I

was sick, and you visited Me; I was in prison, and you came to Me." (vv. 34-36)

These defendants, the sheep, are incredulous. They have never seen Jesus. They are honest enough to say so:

Lord, when did we see You hungry, and feed You, or thirsty, and give You drink? (v. 37)

And they cover all the categories given above by the Lord. They are not aware that they have greatly honored the Lord by their right doings in the Tribulation period.

Jesus explains to them:

Truly I say to you, to the extent that you did it to one of these brothers of Mine, even the least of them, you did it to Me. (v. 40)

The sheep receive full credit for their faith and acts of love during the difficult time of the Antichrist.

Jesus' brethren are the Jews, particularly the 144,000 Jews who suffered the Tribulation period in unflinching faith in the Lord and stalwart witnessing to the lost. In a larger sense, all mankind are Jesus' brethren since He became a man on our behalf. But the context here dictates the "brethen" in question as the Lord's fellow Jews.

Had the sheep been Bible students, they would not have been at all surprised at their acquittal in Jesus' courtroom. God says plainly in Genesis 12:3, at the stirring moment of the Abrahamic covenant, "I will bless those who bless you" (the Jewish nation). As we have seen, God's covenant with His chosen people is to endure to eternity. Jesus would not be expected to condemn those who blessed the Jews.

But God goes on to tell Abraham in that same Scripture, "I will curse them that curse thee," and we now come to the goats, the defendants on Jesus' left.

They failed to exercise benevolence to those in need in the hard times. "For I was hungry, and you gave Me nothing to eat;

I was thirsty, and you gave Me nothing to drink" (Matthew 25:42). They, too, question their Judge: "When did we fail? When did we even *see* You?"

The Lord applies the same precedent:

> Truly I say to you, to the extent that you did not do it to one of the least of these, you did not do it to Me. (v. 45)

They couldn't ask for a fairer trial.

Their sentence is a hard one. They fare no better than the devil and his henchmen. "Depart from Me, accursed ones," pronounces the Lord, "into the eternal fire, which has been prepared for the devil and his angels" (v. 41).

Admission to the millennial kingdom for Gentiles, then, rests on whether they demonstrated faith in Christ by showing kindness to the suffering chosen people in their final hour. There will be some Gentiles, then, who will go through the Tribulation, believe in Christ, and have their hearts in the right place toward the suffering; and so they will obtain a place in the kingdom. They will not become rulers, as age-of-grace Christians will, but they will become subjects in that glorious and peaceful world.

Is there really a person alive who cannot see the good of feeding the hungry, comforting the sick, and clothing the naked? Can Jesus' principles have been so covered over by a relentlessly wicked world that no one will respond in sympathy?

Hardly! The principle of salvation by faith is not relaxed at this remarkable litigation, but an individual might be spared for the smallest show of human mercy. And we all have the potential for mercy. We still are, after all, created in the image of God.

It won't be easy to assist the enemies of the Antichrist in such times. Obviously the punishment on earth will be severe for those who have anything to do with God or His chosen people. The Antichrist is "god" during the Tribulation, as he duly proclaims, and any valid worship of the true God would be a kind of inverse blasphemy.

On the other hand, opportunities to do the right thing will

abound. The vocal 144,000 Hebrew Christian preachers will be a helpless target of the atheistic forces at large in the world. They will likely be jailed, hungry, and otherwise abused. They will certainly need the kind of help the Lord specified for His brethren. At risk of death, courageous believers will still qualify, according to the Scriptures.

And that is how this first judgment day will proceed. Basically we have just two groups—believers, with a free pass into the kingdom, and unbelievers, who will flunk the entrance exam.

Where do *you* stand?

KING OF KINGS

Once the membership of the new kingdom is settled, it gets immediately underway.

Kingdoms on earth never really have worked out very well. Typically, the monarch connived and cheated behind the scenes while the people sang, "God save the king." But it's a completely different story when God *is* the King!

The sinless, compassionate, incorruptible King will make all the difference in the Millennium, despite the fact that, to some degree, men will still be up to their old tricks.

Isaiah gives us an unforgettable picture of the power and abilities of Jesus as King:

> For a child will be born to us, a son will be given to us; And the government will rest on His shoulders; and His name will be called Wonderful Counselor, Mighty God, Eternal Father, Prince of Peace. There will be no end to the increase of His government or of peace on the throne of David, and over His kingdom, to establish it and to uphold it with justice and righteousness from then on and forevermore. The zeal of the LORD of hosts will accomplish this. (9:6-7)

What was not entirely clear to the Jews who read their Scriptures was the two-phase appearance of Jesus on earth. The essence of Christianity—that there was to be first an appearance characterized by the Messiah's rejection and suffering—was overlooked, although it is prophesied clearly (and by the same prophet):

> He was despised and forsaken of men, a man of sorrows, and acquainted with grief. . . . Surely our griefs He Himself bore, and our sorrows He carried. . . . But He was pierced through for our transgressions, He was crushed for our iniquities; the chastening of our well-being fell upon Him, and by His scourging we are healed. All of us like sheep have gone astray, Each of us has turned to his own way; But the LORD has caused the iniquity of us all to fall on Him. (53:3-6)

Somehow, though the kingship of the Messiah was certainly realized by the Jews—they *still* expect their kingly Messiah—His sacrifice aspect was missed, despite this passage and many like it in the Old Testament. Alternate interpretations for these revelations are given by Jewish scholars. But as we have seen, the chosen people are to come to the full realization of their Messiah's mission and will welcome Him as King. Their Promised Land is to become truly the center of the earth.

The necessity of the delay between the Lord's two comings was lost on the Jews, since their Old Testament theology did not reveal a period like the church age. During this period, Christ reaches the world with His gospel. The Jews, already the chosen people, have never felt that they needed this special provision.

The church, as the body of believers reached during the interim period is called, is to marry Jesus before He assumes His earthly throne. John pictures this great wedding in heaven and refers to the church as the bride of Christ (Revelation 19:7).

Following that, Jesus returns with His bride to the earth and occupies His throne of David.

The Christians, then, are originally raptured, or "caught up," to heaven to be with Jesus from the hard times of the Tribulation period on earth, and then they are wed to the Lord. Finally they return with Him and enjoy their promised privileges of ruling in the millennial kingdom. The population of the kingdom is completed when the Christians return with the Lord to join those on the earth who have qualified for the kingdom by their faith in Christ shown by their good works toward the Lord's brethren in the Tribulation. The latter completely qualify as true believers.

Thus, peopled purely with believers, the kingdom will do well and survive a long time. John reveals in Revelation 20 that the kingdom will endure a thousand years, and hence it is called the Millennium (*mille*-thousand; *annum*-year).

PEACE ON EARTH

As King, Jesus achieves what no other ruler has accomplished—peace. For one thousand years the world will experience no war at all.

The Antichrist, with his supernatural powers and huge armies, maintains world peace for a brief period between the Russian invasion of Israel and the Armageddon, but it is the cold war peace we are all familiar with.

Jesus brings the peace foreseen by Isaiah:

> And they will hammer their swords into plowshares, and their spears into pruninghooks. Nation will not lift up sword against nation, and never again will they learn war. (2:4)

The United Nations building in New York City bears a portion of this Scripture on its entrance, but unfortunately it is quoted without the full context. Missing is the first statement of Isaiah 2:4, "And He will judge between the nations." God has been left out, as usual. It is not until the Lord makes His judgments among the nations that the kingdom and its full-time peace will prevail.

How ironic for the world's most celebrated peacemakers to quote from a Book that contains the solutions to all of their problems but fail to read the whole book, or even the whole Scripture that they find suitable.

This world has at least a five-thousand-year history of war with no indications that it will ever be otherwise. Even today, modern man, conqueror of so much disease, tamer of nature,

"THY KINGDOM COME . . . IN EARTH, AS IT IS IN HEAVEN"

explorer of space, still spends most of his time and money fighting. "Defense" claims the riches of every modern nation in proportion to its size, and man's ultimate scientific know-how goes into killing (or, a new term adjusted to our times, overkilling).

The Bible analyzes the problem as a basic maladjustment of men to their Creator and thus to one another. Jesus said, "Peace I leave with you" (John 14:27), and those in relationship to Him know the deepest meaning of this promise. But it will take His very reappearance to accomplish this over the whole of the earth, and then only when the unbelievers have almost killed off their kind.

But Isaiah's fondest visions of peace will be achieved when the Lord returns. Isaiah sees enthusiastic, spiritually motivated people of the world going up to Jerusalem in the Millennium and taking an interest in government:

> Now it will come about that in the last days, the mountain of the house of the LORD will be established as the chief of the mountains [at the Jerusalem temple site[1]] and will be raised above the hills; and all the nations will stream to it. And many peoples will come and say, "Come, let us go up to the mountain of the LORD, to the house of the God of Jacob; that He may teach us concerning His ways, and that we may walk in His paths." For the law will go forth from Zion [Israel], and the word of the LORD from Jerusalem. (2:2-3)

Worthy subjects of a worthy king! Those will be the days!

This remarkable change in world affairs will affect even the animals. They will all become peace-lovers. Isaiah says,

> And the wolf will dwell with the lamb, and the leopard will lie down with the kid, and the calf and the young lion and the fatling together; and a little boy will lead them. . . . The lion will eat straw like the ox. (11:6-7)

1. See Thomas McCall and Zola Levitt, *Satan in the Sanctuary* (Chicago: Moody, 1973) pp. 108-10.

The animals will live together and eat from the fields instead of killing each other as man as done. Even a little child need have no fear of wild animals in the peaceful times to come.

It will be a changed world in more ways than that. No one will die in the Millennium, but children will be born. At first the population will be a little smaller than we are used to, but it will include, along with those we have specified, all the faithful Christians of the church age and the saved Old Testament believers. They will all be resurrected, like their King, and outfitted for immortality.

World history will be a strange subject, if it is discussed at all. It will be exceedingly difficult to convince the children that come along in the happy Millennium that men once hated and killed one another. But the information will be available—particularly in the Bible, which, as we have seen, will be a steady topic of discussion in government circles. The Bible chronicles a lot of man's old ways of doing things, and Jesus observed that heaven and earth would pass away before this best-seller would go out of print. "The earth will be full of the knowledge of the LORD as the waters cover the sea," says Isaiah (11:9).

The twelve apostles will rule over the twelve tribes of Israel, as it enjoys true favored-nation status, and all of those who were "faithful in a very little" (Luke 19:17) will be given great responsibilities under the new regime.

No wonder the Lord urged His followers to pray, "Thy kingdom come!"

WATCH OUT, EGYPT!

The Millennium sounds like a perfect world, but in some small ways it still will not be. Amazingly enough, men will still insist on their rebellious ways, though to quite a lesser degree, even in that ultimate earthly utopia.

The fault lies deeply within the nature of men—in the sin nature they inherited from their common father, Adam. The men born during the Millennium will have the same fatal flaw, and though they will maintain a peaceful world alongside the many believers, some tests of obedience will still be necessary.

Zechariah supplies that the Feast of Tabernacles, commemorating the deliverance of the Hebrew nation from slavery in Egypt to their Promised Land, will still be celebrated each year. And attendance will be mandatory.

> Then it will come about that any who are left of all the nations that went against Jerusalem will go up from year to year to worship the King, the LORD of hosts, and to celebrate the Feast of Booths. And it will be that whichever of the families of the earth does not go up to Jerusalem to worship the King, the LORD of hosts, there will be no rain on them. (Zechariah 14:16-17)

And, as if the Lord knows full well just *who* among the family of nations might fail to appear for the grand old Jewish feast, He says,

> And if the family of *Egypt* does not go not up or enter, then no rain will fall on them; it will be the plague with which the LORD smites the nations who do not go up to celebrate the Feast of Booths. (v. 18, italics added)

And yet again, as if a word to the wise were not going to be sufficient, He warns,

> This will be the punishment of *Egypt*, and the punishment of all the nations who do not go up to celebrate the Feast of Booths. (v. 19, italics added)

If Israel has ever had a dependable enemy it is Egypt, and somehow it appears than even in the Millennium the Egyptians will be loath to offer this simple allegiance to the Lord. Perhaps the Scripture singles out Egypt for emphasis; that is, if Egypt is required to attend, then certainly all the other nations are. We'll have to wait and see.

It makes a peculiar picture. There will be "heathen" in the Millennium as it progresses. Men have always been free, and they will apparently continue to be free to choose God or not.

But they *will* have to render this specified allegiance to Christ once each year. That's hardly as much allegiance as men now pay their respective unbelieving governments. But if they refuse even this small token, they will have some troubles. It's hard to plant when there's no rain—particularly in places like Egypt.

As the centuries pass in the Millennium, and as the population grows, a certain rebellious spirit will foment among the nations. Of course it does not come to war during the Millennium, but at its very end there is something of a replay of the Russian invasion of Israel.

Satan has not been done away with but has been bound helpless for the thousand-year period. At the end of the Millennium he is released for one last try (in effect) at corrupting the world. And he finds armies available.

This final battle is given little space in the Scriptures. John's Revelation covers it in a few verses (20:7-10). Satan is defeated quickly and this time banished to the eternal lake of fire, never to rise up again.

On to Eternity

We can't say much about eternity, because it is a totally supernatural phenomenon. At the end of the Millennium, our story of the coming Russian invasion of Israel is finished; its steady chain of events is finally ended. The world will undergo a change unlike anything since creation.

God will revamp everything. There will be a new heaven, a new earth, and a new Jerusalem. There will be no more time. The oceans will disappear. John reports an incredible scene:

> And I saw a new heaven and a new earth; for the first heaven and the first earth passed away; and there was no longer any sea. And I saw the holy city, new Jerusalem, coming down out of heaven from God, made ready as a bride adorned for her husband. (Revelation 21:1-2)

What kind of picture does that make? Where was John standing? What does a city coming down from the sky look like?

Where did the first heaven and the first earth go?

Obviously, these are matters much beyond the scope of to-day's observer. Perhaps those in the Millennium, who have lived a thousand years and have seen Christ on the earth, will be able to confront such mysteries. There is not space in this little book about war to discuss eternity.

Believers will be there, of course; but heaven only knows (literally!) what form we'll take. We can't live without water, and rain will be needed even in the Millennium, but in eternity there will be a new earth with no seas. We look up at the sky now and think of it as heaven, but that sky is going away somewhere, and a new one will be installed. What is under our feet—the earth—will be something utterly new.

Another judgment will be held for entrance into eternity. This is the famed Judgment Day when Christ will open the book of life and will judge every unbelieving soul who ever walked this earth. The sea will give up her dead, and even hell will be opened to deliver up its dead (Revelation 20:12-13). The billions of souls who inhabited the eons of earthly time will be judged "according to their deeds" one by one!

"And if anyone's name was not found written in the book of life," concludes John, "he was thrown into the lake of fire" (20:15).

7

A Strategy for Christians

Why is God telling us all this?

Did prophecy ever save anybody? Will the fact that Christians quote the Bible about the future impress unbelievers?

Perhaps, but cases in the Bible itself show otherwise. When Jeremiah shouted that the Babylonians were going to destroy Jerusalem and the mighty Temple of God, he was jailed for annoying the government. When Jesus, looking sadly at the great second Temple, said, "Not one stone here shall be left upon another" (Matthew 24:2), He was ridiculed.

Yet, God chose to reveal His plans in advance to those who would read them. What is His purpose? What are we supposed to do?

This chapter is for Christians—those who believe in Jesus and His atoning work. The next chapter is for the unbelievers—practical suggestions for hard times ahead.

We put this one first because the Rapture might come before you finish this book.

We can suggest two reasons that God has chosen to reveal the future. One is timing. As we follow events as they happen, we get a sense of just where we are in God's scheme of things. The other reason is so that we know the alternative to belief in Christ. That alternative is so horrible that it might well spur us on to greater efforts to reach this world for Christ.

This is a late hour for reaching the world, but remember the thief on the cross. He had mere hours to live, but we'll see him in the kingdom!

Christians can relax, if we wish. The rapture will take us off this sinking ship, and we'll be spared further grief. But in the good example of the One who laid down His very life for His friends, we can do better than that.

The apostle gave a word of advice for these times:

> And let us consider how to stimulate one another to love and good deeds, not forsaking our own assembling together, as is the habit of some, but encouraging one another, and all the more, as you see the day drawing near. (Hebrews 10:24-25)

The "day approaching" is the Lord's day—the day when He will commence judging. That day is the fulfillment of prophecy. "So much the more" should we heed this advice as that day approaches.

We are in a much better position than those at the time of the apostles to see that day approaching when it will be too late to help this world. We have our prophecy—our time schedule, as it were. We can check off events as they happen.

When we started to write this book, there was no Yom Kippur War as yet. There was no really reasonable thought of a Russian invasion of Israel in the offing. It would have shocked the world if Russia had invaded Israel at that time.

But a few months later, Russia did shock the world by reportedly mobilizing troops for that war!

We almost ticked off another event in just a few months. May God help us to get this prophecy book to you before it becomes a history book!

Back to the apostle's good advice. Believers are urged not to avoid gathering together and to exhort one another in spiritual graces and good works. We are not to be spiritual hermits, exulting in the fact that our Lord is going to get us out of all this; we are rather to become actively involved with other believers in the wonderful thing that is faith in God.

The effect will be obvious. If believers can show the world a united, triumphant front in these troubled times, it may just cause some of the world to think. They may want to know why we are as we are, and we surely can tell them.

Our churches, our media, and all of our people—Christ's people—need to be stirred up to realize that our Lord gave us a great commission. We are to share the gospel; we are to preach "to every creature" (Mark 16:15).

When John had finished seeing his incredible revelation of the future, with all its stupefying scenes of the last days of this whole creation, he began to witness. In his brief and beautiful way he said,

> And the Spirit and the bride say, "Come." And let the one who hears say, "Come." And let the one who is thirsty come; let the one who wishes take the water of life without cost. (Revelation 22:17)

How fitting a statement: Let him take the water of life freely! In the Millennium, the unbeliever who will not approach the Lord will have no rain. In eternity there is no sea. We have all the water that's left!

If knowing prophecy does not move us to share our faith, something is very wrong. To understand the condition and destiny of literally billions of unsaved people who are plunging headlong toward horrible lives and horrible deaths, to realize through prophecy that the very politics of today's world are rapidly bringing this to pass, to know in addition that a solution to all of this coming agony is readily available to all—to know all that is to be put in a position of most solemn responsibility.

If we know all that and still fail to tell the world at every chance, then we are acting in an unchristian way.

HERE COMES THE BRIDE

The Bride of Christ, the church, the body of believers, is this world's only chance. We must not fail in this. Our God is "not wishing for any to perish" (2 Peter 3:9), and He commissioned us to do the hard work of reaching the lost. The Spirit and the Bride say, "Come."

When we say, "Come," we are extending quite an invitation. We are admitting our friends to the rapture, to the very wedding of Jesus Christ, to the millennial kingdom, and to everlast-

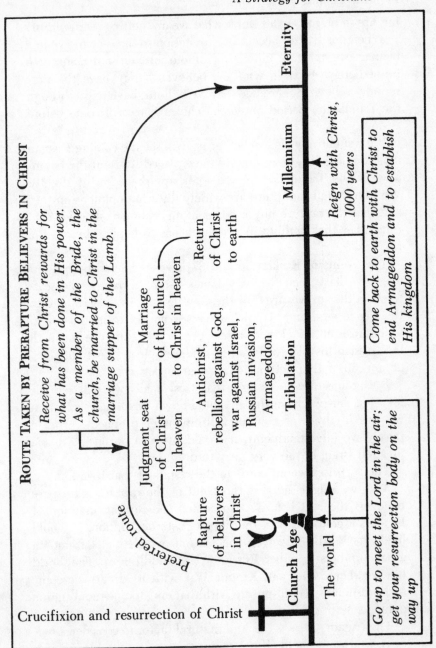

ROUTE TAKEN BY PRERAPTURE BELIEVERS IN CHRIST

Receive from Christ rewards for what has been done in His power.
As a member of the Bride, the church, be married to Christ in the marriage supper of the Lamb.

Eternity

Millennium

Reign with Christ, 1000 years

Return of Christ to earth

Marriage of the church to Christ in heaven

Antichrist, rebellion against God, war against Israel, Russian invasion, Armageddon

Tribulation

Judgment seat of Christ in heaven

Preferred route

Rapture of believers in Christ

Church Age

The world

Crucifixion and resurrection of Christ

Come back to earth with Christ to end Armageddon and to establish His kingdom

Go up to meet the Lord in the air; get your resurrection body on the way up

ing life in eternity. And think what we are getting them *out* of!

When our friends accept our invitation to those coming spectacular events, they inherit all of our heaven-sent assurances immediately. And we who are believers today have the profoundly relieving assurance that we will not have to go through the Tribulation period on earth. The rapture will come before that!

It is not entirely clear whether we will see the coming Russian invasion of Israel, however. We have placed it just at the beginning of the Tribulation period—perhaps preceding it slightly. We have stated that there are widely differing opinions on this, and that the rapture might occur at any moment. It is good to remember that nothing in prophecy has to happen before the rapture.

The events of Ezekiel 36 and 37 have happened before our eyes. We have seen the "dry bones"—the Jewish people scattered in the "graveyards" of the Gentile nations—regathered to the Promised Land. We have seen a nation form there and maintain itself for close to a half century. Ezekiel goes on with the Russian invasion of Israel immediately in his next chapters, 38 and 39, noting nothing to happen in between.

It is conjecture to assume that this means we will see the invasion, but we have the advantage over past analysts in that we live in times of evident fulfillment of prophecy. From a purely worldly standpoint, it would surprise no one if Russia invaded Israel in the very near future.

The surprises would come in the results of that invasion.

Also, we might say that the point of the rapture is to spare believers the real holocaust to come. The Russian invasion of Israel is a confined war, by the prophet's description. It would likely have little effect on the church, which is not found in great numbers in either Russia or the Middle East. The world has weathered the Yom Kippur War with its dreary outcome and presumably could put up with that one, too, without undue damage.

Then again, there is the supernatural factor to consider. Logically, God would hold off the rapture as long as possible in order to gather as many souls to the harvest as He can. But He acts in a visible way in the Russian invasion. We have seen that fire comes down on the Russian armies, and unless this description relates to nuclear attack or something we can understand in an earthly way, God would be "exposing" Himself to the world.

It is held by many commentators that when God actually shows Himself by His actions, the age of faith is over.

In any case, we hold that the rapture and the Russian invasion of Israel are close together, near the beginning of the Tribulation period. If we are right in that, signs of the Russian invasion are virtually signs of the rapture.

During that scary Yom Kippur week when the Russians reportedly were mobilizing troops, we seemed to be very close to fulfilling end-times prophecy. That a situation very like that seen by Ezekiel could happen in these times certainly suggests that the fulfillment of his visions is quite possible—and maybe very close.

So, in a way, we are rapidly becoming friends in need to our unbelieving fellow men. It's no longer a question of "Come to our church," but more like "Avoid the Antichrist and Armageddon."

Our knowledge, which the Lord has imparted to us, is of inestimable value to the world. If we withhold it, we would be like researchers withholding a cure for cancer. We have the truth, and as our Lord said, "The truth shall make you free" (John 8:32).

We can calculate the timing of God's plan by watching our world. We can see the alternatives to going with God by just reading the prophecy in the Bible.

The strategy for Christians has been disclosed:

> And Jesus came up and spoke to them, saying, "All authority has been given to Me in heaven and on earth. Go therefore and make disciples of all the nations, baptizing them in the name of the Father and the Son and the Holy Spirit, teaching them to observe all that I commanded you; and lo, I am with you always, even to the end of the age." (Matthew 28:18-20)

8

A Strategy for Unbelievers

Perhaps, however, you do not believe in Christ, and we have not persuaded you. Perhaps you have found this book to be good bedtime reading and an entertaining theory of things to come, but you figure you'll make out on your own wits as you always have.

Very well. First, please know that we love you.

We don't mean to sound fatuous, but we'd hardly be good representatives of Jesus Christ on earth if we failed to love all men as He commanded. But it is not just a matter of following His dictum. We are *able* to love you. Christianity has the peculiar effect of inbuing the plainest individuals with a real ability to love—even to love enemies, as our Lord also counseled. We do not regard you as an enemy, but rather a brother—a brother in great need.

So, if you will, we would like to make a few suggestions about the future. In view of all of the coming circumstances we have outlined, we think you should take action.

First of all, the Bible itself gives one imperative to unbelievers. "Believe on the Lord Jesus Christ, and thou shalt be saved" (Acts 16:31). We would be remiss to leave that out. We think it's still the only way to go.

Failing that, let's consider reasonable alternatives. Since the coming Russian invasion of Israel appears to be in preparation these days, and since that seems to start the whole chain of tragic events associated with the end times, you'd better get moving!

Discussing the effects of the abortive Russian invasion, Ezekiel specifies that there will be fire on Magog and among those who dwell securely in the coastlands (see 39:6). This cryptic "coastlands" is more easily understood when we look at it in the context of Ezekiel's world. In that Mediterranean area, most countries were more densely settled along their coasts to facilitate trade. Ships were the ultimate tool of international commerce. The present United States is still an example of more densely settled coastlands than inland areas. Ezekiel's term indicated the civilizations across the seas from Israel.

It is possible, then, that we Americans are counted among those "who dwell securely in the coastlands" and that this "fire" capable of wiping out the enormous allied forces of the Russian invasion will have its effects elsewhere. This is especially reasonable when we consider the overwhelming destruction of nuclear warfare and its resulting fallout.

Therefore, it would be good if you would now install a bomb shelter capable of resisting atomic-scale warfare and radiation. People may think you're a bit paranoid, but they also laughed at Noah until it started to rain.

Fortunately, although the destruction resulting from the Russian invasion appears to be very widespread, it's over quickly, and the world goes on. Let us assume you have taken our advice about the bomb shelter and have survived. What next?

Next you should watch for the rapture of the church. This will be unmistakable. The Christians will simply disappear. Since they are to meet the Lord in the air, they will just be "gone" all at once. There's been a lot of conjecture about how this will happen and how it will be explained, but remember, we are dealing here with a period of divine activity, and lots of things are going to seem strange.

Conceivably, those two events—the invasion and the rapture—will be in the other order, as we have explained, but in any case, they'll be close together.

The one or the other may make a believer out of you. Jonah, who resisted the Lord's directives, had a definite change of heart when he came back out of the great fish! But assuming that your faith in godlessness still persists, you are in for the long ride. Once the rapture has occurred, your chance to be airlifted out of all this is over. You can always still revert to Christ, but you'll have your troubles!

The next thing to watch for is the appearance of the Antichrist. This will occur right after the rapture and, we think, right after the Russian invasion.

If you are a typical unbeliever of that day, you will say to the Antichrist, "Thank you. At last we're going to have peace"; and you will bow down to that glib egomaniac like all the others. You will note with distaste a continuing Christian activity, but you will be delighted to participate in the new regime of the Tribulation period. You'll gladly have your number tattooed on your skin so that you can go shopping conveniently; and you'll think the world has at last pulled itself together.

Memories of this book and many others that warned about such things may come to your mind from time to time, but you'll think, "Those fellows had no appreciation for what men can accomplish when they get together."

The joke is on you!

You'll sigh with gladness over the peace in the Middle East, and you'll watch the Tribulation Temple, a truly magnificent piece of architecture, rise in Jerusalem. You will probably think, "You have to give those Jews credit. They really hang in there. When the going gets tough, the tough get going." (The Temple might be actually constructed ahead of these other events, but, in any case, it will be standing and functioning by the middle of the Tribulation period.)

You'll watch with approval, if you are a typical unbeliever, as the Antichrist signs a treaty with Israel; and it will seem to you that the troublesome powder keg will at last be permanently defused.

But getting back to our suggestions for you, that treaty-signing will start your last seven years, and you should act accordingly. It might be best to sell everything you have and get really far away from the Middle East. You're on your way to Armageddon.

You may chance across a witness for Christ at this late date.

He may be one of those 144,000 preachers of Israel, and you may find him appealing for his very stubbornness and courage under fire.

May we recommend him to you? It still won't be too late. He'll provide you safe passage to the Millennium if you'll believe.

But you may resist him because belief in Christ will be a very risky proposition at that point. The Antichrist will have everybody computerized, and the remaining Christians will be on the most stupendous "enemies list" of all time. You may want to avoid that. You'll see Christians actually executed for their faith.

Frankly, we would encourage you to take this life-and-death risk. If you come to believe in the Lord Jesus, you will pass into the new kingdom. If you do not, sooner or later you will die forever. To resist out of fear would be to trade eternity for less than seven years of the worst possible earthly life. In this particular case, you are truly worth more dead than alive.

But at least be kind to that Hebrew Christian preacher. Remember, Jesus will take that behavior into consideration in the immigration office of the Millennium. If you have the chance to feed a starving Jew, or to clothe him, or to comfort him while he is sick or in prison, for your own sake do so! Become a sheep and be separated from the goats!

Eventually you will see the Antichrist go into the new Jerusalem Temple and proclaim himself God. This may strike you as a bit egotistical, but we have tolerated such excesses in our leaders before. You'll probably go along with it.

At all costs, resist having the identifying number stamped on you, if it has not been done already. You may go hungry for a while because you will not be able to go through the checkout line at the local supermarket without your number, but you'll be better off foraging for food than being judged later on. It's not quite clear when that particular legislation will take place, but even under the Antichrist's computerized systems, it will take some time to number everybody in the world. You may have a chance to hold off. By all means, do so!

But if you go along with this too, your alternatives have really

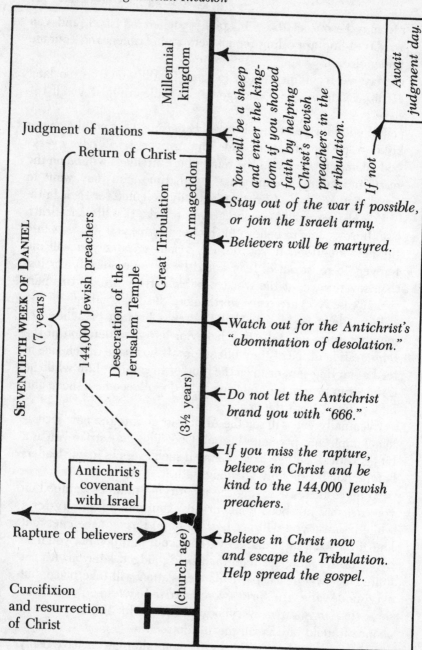

Await judgment day.

Millennial kingdom

Judgment of nations

Return of Christ

You will be a sheep and enter the kingdom if you showed faith by helping Christ's Jewish preachers in the tribulation.

If not

Armageddon

Great Tribulation

Stay out of the war if possible, or join the Israeli army.

Believers will be martyred.

SEVENTIETH WEEK OF DANIEL (7 years)

144,000 Jewish preachers

Desecration of the Jerusalem Temple

Watch out for the Antichrist's "abomination of desolation."

(3½ years)

Do not let the Antichrist brand you with "666."

Antichrist's covenant with Israel

If you miss the rapture, believe in Christ and be kind to the 144,000 Jewish preachers.

Rapture of believers

(church age)

Believe in Christ now and escape the Tribulation. Help spread the gospel.

Curcifixion and resurrection of Christ

run out. Assuming that you bear the Antichrist's number, have not taken the opportunity to be kind to the brethren of the Lord, and still do not believe in Jesus Christ, everything else will be done *for* you.

If you have never had the opportunity to visit Israel, you will go at government expense when you are drafted into the Antichrist's army. If you can, you should seek high ground in Israel because of virtual seas of blood as high as the bridles of the horses. If you can make yourself scarce enough to survive the demolishing of the Gentile forces by Jesus and His heavenly army, you will make it as far as the trial before the throne of Christ. But you will be a goat, and the verdict will be "eternal punishment" (Matthew 25:46).

We are not threatening you. We're just quoting the Book that contains all the rest of our information. We've seen too much of it come true to doubt it at this point.

We don't know precisely what that everlasting punishment will be, but we know about the alternative. Bear with us a little longer, while we explain.

A More Excellent Way

To quote a phrase from Scripture, "Behold, I show you a more excellent way."

Anything would be "more excellent" than the way the Bible says things are going to be for unbelievers. The alternative to the end times holocaust is so pleasant and so simply attained that we feel we must say it one last time, complete with the method.

Believers, as we have seen, will see the rapture, the Millennium, and eternity, rather than destruction and punishment. You can become a believer virtually at once.

The Lord's attitude on your salvation is clear: "I stand at the door and knock" (Revelation 3:20). "He is not wishing for any to perish" (2 Peter 3:9). "But as many as received Him, to them He gave the right to become children of God" (John 1:12).

Approaching God is quite a natural thing. He is, after all, the Creator of nature. There is hardly a thinking person anywhere who cannot see that nature has a Maker and that the affairs of this world give the impression of having a plan. Supplied further with the truths of prophecy and the fact that they are coming to pass, the unbeliever can readily approach God without feeling strange.

You do not have to write or phone. God has indicated that He will hear you whatever your circumstances, wherever you are.

You do not have to be anybody special. Jesus had time for the lepers and thieves as well as for the mighty and powerful. You do not have to qualify in any special social group; the tax collectors and prostitutes go into heaven before the befrocked high priests of Israel, according to Jesus.

You do not have to change yourself; God delights in taking care of that in return for your faith. You will be a happier, kinder, more loving individual, as you have always wanted to be, when Christ takes over your life.

And you will get the world's best "buyer protection plan." You will live on and on in joy and peace, avoiding the terrible ending of this world as we know it and proceeding to the best of all possible worlds.

In talking to God, use your own words. He knows you, and there's no use putting up a false front.

You might try saying something on this order:

Lord Jesus, I believe that You died for me and can give me everlasting life. Please do this for me and let me live for You from now on. Thanks.

Do it now. And we'll see you in the kingdom!

Update: 1987

With the benefit of hindsight, those who have read *The Coming Russian Invasion of Israel* can see that there is nothing to retract. The book follows the predictions of Ezekiel 37-39 exactly, and world events have only corroborated the prophecy and helped bring its fulfillment into focus. No predictions made in the original volume need to be corrected, but much can be added at this point. Here is a brief overview of Ezekiel's picture of the invasion put in the form of the events transpiring with each participating nation.

LIBYA (PUT)

Libya is a sparsely populated desert dictatorship that in fifteen years has come from a pre-feudal society to become one of the most menacing enemies of Israel. It has been foremost in the news (1986) in view of Colonel Muammar Qaddafi's rabidly anti-Israeli, anti-American, and pro-terroristic stance. Nothing would please this regime more than to cooperate in a massive international invasion of Israel.

To this end, Qaddafi has been establishing a closer relationship with Russia, and it has even been said that he seeks a power-sharing arrangement with the Communists. He has boasted on international television about "aligning with Russia" and, Hitler-like, has referred to Americans as "sub-human." He wants to vent a terrible anger, and he can't take on the United States alone. Israel is smaller and closer and, he thinks, weaker. A fomenter of terrorism, he already has targeted Israel in the past.

Libya is given as an ally of Russia in the invasion in Ezekiel 38:5.

MAGOG (RUSSIA)

This book details the identification of modern Russia with the biblical power of Magog. Russia is the superpower that has backed the Muslim nations with armaments for the purpose of annihilating Israel over the past thirty years. The atheistic USSR came perilously close to direct intervention near the close of the Yom-Kippur war (1973) when an Egyptian army was surrounded in the Sinai.

Russia may be concluding at this point that the Arab nations are simply not going to get the job done. Israel has become a significant power relative to its neighbors and in the Russian thinking may require superpower intervention. Russia supports Libya in general and deeply resents the democracy of Israel in the Middle East.

The Russians have had their hands full with the Chernobyl disaster and its aftermath. On the Chicago commodities market, wheat prices shot up the day after the reactor explosion. Russia's food belt was badly damaged. Wheat will be needed because of the poisoned soil in the area of the calamity, and cattle are being slaughtered because they are diseased. The agricultural production of the territory surrounding the accident may be spoiled forever. Ezekiel lays stress on the fact that Israel is a land of great herds of cattle (38:12, 14, etc.). It is far and away the best food producer of the Middle East and, in fact, achieves better food yield per acre than any nation in the world, including the United States. In addition to its food problems, Russia has a need for warm water ports, improved air fields, and control of the level of technology that Israel possesses to continue its expansionist political policies.

The Russians may well be thinking that the precedent for a superpower invasion of a small Middle-Eastern nation was established by the American bombing run on Libya in April 1986. Magog (Russia) is given as the leader of the invasion in Ezekiel 38:2.

PERSIA (IRAN)

An ally of the United States and of Israel in 1974, Iran has descended into a backward society of fanatical Muslim reactionaries. Under Khomeini, Iran is viciously anti-Israeli and anti-American and suffers from an exhausting five-year war with its Muslim neighbor, Iraq. Presently, Iran is cultivating relations with the Soviet Union, and it is clear that its ultimate purposes would be best served by overrunning Israel and capturing Jerusalem, with its important Muslim shrines. The Russians would welcome the participation of this eastern flank power in an invasion of Israel.

Persia (Iran) is given as an ally of Russia in the invasion in Ezekiel 38:5.

ETHIOPIA

Ethiopia is another case of a nation's radically changing its alliances and its philosophy since the writing of this book. Formerly a monarchy under Emperor Haile Selassie, Ethiopia was definitely pro-Israel. The emperor styled himself "the lion of the tribe of Judah" and imagined that he was the descendant of a liaison between King Solomon and the Queen of Sheba. Ethiopia contained large numbers of Jewish people, who have since emigrated to the Promised Land. The government turned Marxist shortly after the original publication of this book and has since deteriorated catastrophically. Stunned by famine, the Ethiopians can only take direction from their masters in Moscow. Ethiopia has actually become a most vocal critic of Israel. Russia could well use a southern flank attacker of Israel. That assault would create a diversion from the primarily northern invasion forces and compel the Israelis to divide their defensive strength.

Ethiopia is given as an ally of Russia in the invasion in Ezekiel 38:5.

GOMER, TOGARMAH

The tribal names *Gomer* and *Togarmah* appear to include the nations from Turkey up through the Warsaw Pact countries of

Eastern Europe, as the book details. These territories take their orders from the Kremlin now and will certainly do so in the time of the invasion. The original names appear in Genesis 10:1, and the appearance of nations hostile to Israel in these very geographical areas corroborates the prophecy.

Gomer and Togarmah are given as allies of Russia in the invasion in Ezekiel 38:6.

SHEBA, DEDAN

When the Russian invasion occurs, Sheba and Dedan, nations of the Arabian peninsula, will raise objections. These probably include the oil rich kingdom of Saudi Arabia, whose Vienna airline headquarters was targeted by Qaddafi in a terrorist attack in April 1986. They are observers of the invasion and not participants in it.

Their objections are detailed in Ezekiel 38:13, where they supply a reason for Russia's aggression—"to take away cattle and goods, to take a great spoil."

"THE YOUNG LIONS"

Also raising objections to the invasion are those identified as "the young lions." Some have speculated that these might represent Great Britain, with its lion emblem, and its political offspring, the United States. If so, this would be one of the few, if any, passages of Scripture where these modern church age nations are referenced. In any case, there is no clear participation of Western nations in the invasion itself, primarily because their help seems not to be needed. The God of Israel will settle the fray literally before they can attend to the battlefield. The United States, at any rate, has already helped arm Israel to fend off just such an invasion.

The objections of the young lions to the invasion are detailed in Ezekiel 38:13.

EGYPT, LEBANON, SYRIA, JORDAN

In modern politics we are used to thinking of the close neighbors of Israel—Egypt, Lebanon, Syria, and Jordan—as being her most dangerous enemies. But none of these bordering powers are mentioned in Ezekiel's description. They have all been active in the various wars against Israel since 1948, but in the example of Egypt we can see a remarkable peace process. For the first time in 4,000 years, Pharaoh came to Jerusalem in peace. The Camp David treaty of 1977 has taken hold and is being observed scrupulously, at least insofar as bearing arms is concerned. Similar peace treaties are signed between warring factions in Beirut year in and year out with no such effect. Will the Almighty pacify these other enemies of Israel as well before the invasion takes place? Or will Russia overestimate its strength so drastically as to omit asking for their help?

CONCLUDING THOUGHTS

Considering all of the above, no Bible reader should be surprised if the Russian invasion of Israel happens very soon. And, of course, the rapture of the church would most probably precede it. The rapture is not attached to any prophetic event but is a free-floating and imminent issue. It can happen at any time, but it is clear that if the world is to go into a divinely interrupted catastrophe like an attempted full-scale invasion of Israel, then the church age is at an end. People would then not "believe in things not seen," but rather they would believe by sight. This is more characteristic of the Tribulation period than the age of grace, and therefore the rapture should precede the invasion.

The Antichrist's covenant would logically immediately follow the repulsed invasion, since Israel, having been surprised and delivered, would be in a posture to accept terms of peace.

Epilogue

Our updated book is now finished. But the story told here and the prophecies we have studied are not finished. Rather, they keep moving inexorably ahead toward the fateful climax described in these pages.

We have not needed to retract one line of anything we wrote more than a decade ago about the coming future war, but, on the contrary, our suggested views about events have been repeatedly confirmed. Why have we been so persistently vindicated?

Do we have connections with world leaders in high places? No. Do we have access to information not available to the general public? No. Are we prophets? Do we have psychic powers or are we smarter than others? No.

We simply believe, with as much childlike faith as possible, what was written by the Lord's prophet Ezekiel so many centuries ago and can be read by anyone who possesses a copy of the Bible.

Our sole contribution has been to cast a spotlight on what the prophet wrote and to show how events in our time in regathered Israel, Russia, Europe, and the Middle East fit perfectly into the pattern described by Ezekiel for the latter days. The reader must judge for himself if our comparisons are obvious and accurate or in any way strained or forced. Whatever our opinions, God's prophetic word will be accomplished to the letter, and that is the heart of our message.

What will the next decade bring? Will there be more stage setting for the end times, as we have seen the last few years? Or will the schedule accelerate with the rapture of the church, the Russian invasion of Israel, the Tribulation, and the second coming of Christ? All of that could occur in the same span of time that has elapsed since the first edition of this book was published.

We do not know the day or the hour, and we are commanded to leave all matters concerning the timing of the prophetic events in the Lord's hands without attempt at calculation. What we do know is that the Lord's coming and these events are "nearer than when we first believed," and with that hope we urge our readers to wait patiently and energetically for the soon return of the One who loved us and died for us.